# Luck of the Draw

## NED MANNING

**CURRENCY PRESS**
The performing arts publisher

CURRENCY PLAYS

First published in 2000
by Currency Press Pty Ltd,
Gadigal Land, Suite 310, 46-56 Kippax Street, Surry Hills NSW 2010 Australia
enquiries@currency.com.au
www.currency.com.au

NATIONAL LIBRARY OF AUSTRALIA CIP DATA
Manning, Ned, 1950–.
Luck of the draw.
ISBN 9780868196350.
1. Aborigines, Australian—Families—Drama. 2. Aborigines, Australian—
Treatment—Drama. I. Kooemba Jdarra (Theatrical company). II. Title.
(Series: Current theatre series).
A822.3

Typeset by Erin Dewar for Currency Press.
Cover design by Katy Wall for Currency Press.
Currency Press acknowledges the Traditional Owners of the Country on which
we live and work. We pay our respects to all Aboriginal and Torres Strait
Islander Elders, past and present.

# Contents

# FORWARD

As if our life were a jigsaw puzzle, we need each precious piece of this puzzle before the picture becomes complete. It is my belief that this 'completeness' will only be achieved once each and every one of us embarks on a journey of self-discovery—a journey that will help us, in our own mind's eye, to recognise who we are as a person. Sometimes this journey may be painful for some, and joyous for others; however, unless this process of self-discovery is undertaken, we will continue living our lives with many questions unanswered and our lives full of gaps.

As a Murri woman, I am all too well aware of this need to find the missing pieces of one's life. Due to past government policies Murri people were forcibly removed from their homes, children were taken, and lives were controlled. At school, on a government controlled settlement, our Social Studies books contained pictures of Aboriginal people from Central Australia implying that they were the 'true' Indigenous people. And so as a child, I had often wondered, 'If those people were Aboriginal, then who are we—those of us living on Settlements and Missions?'

*Luck of the Draw* poignantly deals with this issue of self-discovery and I congratulate both its director and writer for the way in which they have captured this theme. It is hoped that you will walk away from this play either in the knowledge that you have already found all of those 'missing pieces' and can admire the completed masterpiece. Or you will join those of us who are in desperate search of our roots and seeking answers to those haunting questions: 'Where did I come from?', but more importantly, 'Where do I belong?'

*Mrs Lesley Williams*
*Gympie, Queensland*
*3 June 2000*

# PLAYWRIGHT'S NOTE

*Luck of the Draw* began life when I revisited another play, *Close to the Bone*, with the intention of rewriting what was essentially a play for school students and making it 'closer to the bone'. It was motivated by a desire to confront the issues dealing with Aboriginality and White Australia's response to those issues in the post-war period. Where *Close to the Bone* sugar-coated some of these issues for the obvious reason that it was aimed at primary and secondary school students, I felt a need in the current political climate to deal with these issues head on.

I, therefore, owe an enormous debt of gratitude to the students at the EORA Centre in Redfern who set me on this path over ten years ago. However, a play needs to be a play and not a political treatise and ultimately this play will stand or fall because of its theatrical worth. To that end I would like to acknowledge the input and encouragement I received from Ruth Little and Marion Potts, both of whom provided dramaturgical advice.

I must also acknowledge the support I have received from the Darwin Theatre Company and Kooemba Jdarra.

*Ned Manning*
*May 2000*

*Luck of the Draw* was first produced by Darwin Theatre Company and performed at the Browns Mart Theatre, Darwin, on 6 May 1999, with the following cast:

| | |
|---|---|
| ANNIE | Tessa Rose |
| PEARL | Suzanne Clarke |
| PAT | Ronald Love |
| NELL | Tegan Richardson |
| BRIAN / JOE | Joseph Clements |
| WELFARE OFFICER | Mark Bunnett |

Director, Richard Mellick
Sets & Costumes Designer, Louise Carmichael
Production Manager & Lighting Designer, Anne-Marie Garcia
Stage Manager, Beryl Brugmans

## CHARACTERS

ANNIE

PEARL

PAT / BLACKIE

NELL / MATRON

JOE / BRIAN / REG

# ACT ONE

## SCENE ONE

*1944. Night. A railway station in a country town.*

*An Aboriginal* MAN, *dressed in the uniform of the Australian Imperial Forces, stands with arms outstretched in front of a steam train. He is silhouetted against the train's spotlight. The train's whistle rings out as the engine begins to crank up. He is* PAT *and* ANNIE*'s father.* REG *is* JOE*'s father and* MATRON *is from the Aboriginal Protection Board. A female voice calls out.*

MATRON: Hold on!

> *Another blast from the whistle.*

Stop the train! For God's sake, stop the train!

> *A male voice replies.*

REG: What's goin' on?

MATRON: There's something on the track…

REG: Eh?

MATRON: Hell's bells! There's a bloke…

REG: Gawd Almighty! Hey, Blackie! What do think you're doing?

MATRON: Who is it?

REG: Blackie Dodd. You've got his kids in there.

MATRON: You better shift him.

REG: Come on, mate, get off the bloody track!

MATRON: Hurry up!

REG: He's got his feet wedged against the sleepers…

MATRON: Get down there and move him, you bloody dill. He's trying to stop the train.

> REG *jumps onto the track and grabs the* MAN*'s arm. He drags him* (BLACKIE) *off.*

REG: Come on, Blackie, don't be silly.

BLACKIE: No…

*Another blast from the whistle. The noise of the train is deafening. The harsh spotlight blinds the audience.* BLACKIE*'s screams are heard offstage.*

No!

MATRON *looks down the track and finally signals for the train to move off.*

◆ ◆ ◆ ◆ ◆

*SCENE TWO*

*1955. Day. The same railway station eleven years later.*

*A young Aboriginal girl,* ANNIE, *14, stands on the platform. She looks out as if trying to spot something in the distance. She looks around.*

ANNIE: Come on, Pat! [*She takes a coin out of her pocket at spins it into the air.*] Heads we go that way. Tails we go that way. [*She catches it and slaps it onto the back of her hand.*] Heads. That way!

*Her brother* PAT, *17, enters carrying suitcases.*

PAT: No luck. We'll have to walk.

ANNIE: Walk?

PAT: Yeah. Not far. [*He takes a big, deep breath.*] Breathe that in. That sea air! Bewdiful! Gets the old lungs goin', doesn't it? Smell that salt? Ohhh… been longin' for this moment! Hey! Come on, like this…

*He demonstrates.* ANNIE *follows.*

Through your nose… great big breath… that's the shot! Great, isn't it?

ANNIE: Yeah…

PAT: It's great all right. Great! Nothin' like it in the whole world. Kept me goin' it has. Just the thought of comin' back here. Our place. Good, eh? Good to be home at last.

ANNIE *stares blankly ahead.*

What's the matter?

ANNIE: Nothing.

PAT: Cheer up! That mob won't find us here, sis. Hey! Look! [*He balances on a suitcase to get a better view.*] See there?

ANNIE: Where?

PAT: There.

> *He helps her up.*

That there, sis. That's our Special Place. See the river? She runs into the sea behind that headland there. That's where the salt water and the fresh water meet.

ANNIE: Can't see…

PAT: Headland either side, lots of little bays… the beach over there… that's the place I been dreamin' of. I tell you what, sis. That place there… we used to dive for mussels there, eh?! When you were real little. Hangin' on to that big rock there, divin' down and fillin' up a sugar bag. Jeez it was fun. Dad reckoned it was a perfect spot 'cause the river water and sea water all swirled around with the current and the tide. Tell you what though, if the tide was runnin' you had to hang on tight or the current'd sweep you out to sea, quick as a flash!

ANNIE: Can we go?

PAT: Sis, she'll be right. Trust me.

ANNIE: I'm scared.

PAT: What for?

> ANNIE *looks down the track.*

No one comin'!

ANNIE: You sure?

PAT: Jeez, sis, the last few days we've covered half the bloody country! How could they track us here? They don't know where we come from. Prob'ly don't even know we're related. We're safe as the bank here.

> ANNIE *starts crying.*

Now don't start bawlin' on me.

ANNIE: What about this one? [*She pats her stomach.*] I wanted to remember. So I could tell this one here. I thought it'd all come back. Soon as we got off the train I thought… I hoped… but I can't remember anything. I only got what you told me.

PAT: You listen to me, sis. This place is in your blood. It'll come back. Just you wait and see. Once you get around a bit.

ANNIE: Will you help me?

PAT: 'Course I will.

ANNIE: Show me everything?

PAT: Sure.

ANNIE: We'll stick together, eh?

PAT: Yeah.

ANNIE: Good.

PAT: After I get back.

ANNIE: Get back?

PAT: I'll get you settled into the 'Mish' and then… I've got to go out west, Goondiwindi way.

ANNIE: You can't…

PAT: There's good drovin' work there. Beautiful horses they reckon. It's not that far. I'll keep in touch.

ANNIE: I don't know anyone…

PAT: Don't worry about that. You will. Plenty of family 'round here. You'll be right. Someone's got to earn a quid for the bub, eh? Till you get on your feet. Come on, sis. I won't let you down. Got you out of that Girl's Home, didn't I?

ANNIE: Can't you stay for a week or two?

PAT: As soon as I make enough dough I'll be back. Then I'll show you how to get them mussels, eh? Cheer up, you'll be jake. Eh? Go on. Don't be such a sourpuss. Oi! Think of that bloody old Matron runnin' 'round like a blue-arsed fly wonderin' where the hell you got to!

ANNIE: Yeah…

PAT: 'Where's Number Sixty-Two?' she'll be yellin' out. 'Where's Sixty-Two?'

ANNIE: Bloody old bitch.

PAT: That's more like it! A bit of the old Dodd spirit, eh? Come on. Let's make tracks.

ANNIE: You never said how far it was.

PAT: Oh, about… can't really remember… about ten miles or so.

ANNIE: Ten miles!

PAT: We should get there before dark if we get a rattle on…

ANNIE *sits on a suitcase.*

What're you doin'?

ANNIE: I'm not walkin' nowhere.

PAT: Don't be silly. 'Course you're gonna walk.

ANNIE: You can walk! I'm stayin' here.

PAT: Oh, for God's sake…

ANNIE: Two days on that train, all that galloping…

PAT: How'd you expect me to get you out? In a bloody Rolls Royce!

ANNIE: … this one needs a blow and so do I.

PAT: You get off your bloody arse and get cracking.

JOE, *a young man about* PAT*'s age, runs on.*

JOE: G'day.

PAT: Oh, g'day.

JOE: Here yet?

PAT: Eh?

JOE: The train.

PAT: She's gone, mate.

JOE: Gone? Don't tell me I missed her?

PAT: Looks that way.

JOE: Bugger it! Seen the station master?

PAT: Nuh. Place's deserted.

JOE: Oh, shit! 'Course! Footy's on, home game. Couldn't give us hand, could you?

PAT: What's up?

JOE: Axle's snapped.

PAT: Oh?

JOE: Got a big load of sleepers on. Slipped down the bank…

PAT: Uh-huh.

JOE: The old man'll kill me.

PAT: Yeah?

JOE: He's the station master.

PAT: Right.

JOE: Won't be happy.

PAT: No.

ANNIE: Tell you what, we'll do you a deal.

JOE: Eh?

ANNIE: We'll give you a hand and you can give us a lift out to the Mission.

JOE: Told ya, got a load o' logs… not much room…

ANNIE: He won't mind, will you, bro?

PAT: Hang about. I'm gonna fix the bloody axle and as a reward I get to sit on the load while you sit up like Jacky in the front.

ANNIE: That's right. 'Cept I'll be sittin' up like Jilly, eh? Annie's me name. He's Pat. Now, where's these sleepers?

JOE: Down there.

ANNIE: Knew it was that way!

> *She grabs the bags and heads off.*

JOE: Pat?

PAT: Yeah…

JOE: Pat Dodd?

PAT: Mmm.

JOE: Crikey.

PAT: What?

JOE: Bugger me dead. You don't remember, do you? It's me. Joe. Remember? We used to play down the creek when we was kids. You used to dive-bomb us from the big willow tree. Reckoned you were a Spitfire. No one could ever catch you. Then youse just disappeared.

PAT: Yeah.

JOE: Where you been all these years?

PAT: Out west. On a big cattle station. With family.

JOE: Right-oh.

PAT: Decided to come back.

JOE: Don't blame you. Best spot in the world this.

PAT: Missed the sea.

ANNIE: [*calling out*] Come on, you two. There's work to be done!

PAT: Better have a look at this axle then.

JOE: Fair enough.

PAT: Over there, is it?

JOE: Yeah. Near the cheese factory.

PAT: Race you?

JOE: Eh?

PAT: Loser rides on the load.

JOE: You're on!

> *They race off.*

◆ ◆ ◆ ◆ ◆

## SCENE THREE

*1956 The Mission.*

ANNIE *folds nappies, rocking a bassinette with her foot.*

ANNIE: There. That's better. That's a good girl. Go to sleep now. Mummy's got all those beautiful plums to stew up. Yes she has. Lots of big, juicy plums. Beautiful! That's what's so good about this place, bub. Plenty of fresh tucker, eh? Not like that lousy Home and all that rotten porridge. What's that? Reckon it shows? Reckon I'm putting on weight? [*She checks herself out.*] What are you grinning at? You're meant to be asleep. You laughin' at your silly mummy?! Just you wait, you're going to love it here, you are. Down the swimming hole, swinging off the rope, having lots of fun. You're the luckiest girl in the world and the most beautiful. Yes you are! You're the most beautiful girl in the whole wide world.

*She rocks the bassinette, humming a lullaby.*

Nigh' night,
Sleepy tight,
Time to say goodnight tonight.

*She repeats this until the baby is asleep.*

When you get older you're gonna learn all about this place. All the stuff I never learnt. You're gonna learn it all. So you know. So no one can take it away from you. Oh yes, all the songs and all the stories, all that stuff. You're gonna learn everything. And you're gonna learn your school work too. Yes you are. You're gonna be on the top of the tree. That's my girl. We're gonna make sure you get the best of everything, we are. [*She sits.*] That old bastard never knew what he was doing when he got me pregnant. He gave me something to live for he did.

◆ ◆ ◆ ◆ ◆

## SCENE FOUR

*1963. The Mission. Night.*

PEARL, *nearly 8, spins a coin imitating two-up. It's a World War Two medal.*

PEARL: Heads. Tails. Heads. Tails. Tails. Tails.

    *She hides the medal and grabs a book as* ANNIE *enters.*

ANNIE: Beautiful tomatoes, eh?

PEARL: Mmm.

ANNIE: I tell you what, girl, no one grows tomatoes like your mother. What are you up to?

PEARL: Nothing.

ANNIE: You sure?

PEARL: Yeah!

ANNIE: Done your homework?

PEARL: Yes, Mum.

ANNIE: Good girl. Where you up to?

PEARL: The bit where 'Ginger' dies.

ANNIE: Oh.

PEARL: She won't do as she's told.

ANNIE: And 'Beauty'?

PEARL: She's a good horse.

ANNIE: Which is your favourite?

PEARL: 'Black Beauty' of course!

    ANNIE *holds up a big, red tomato.*

ANNIE: Look at that, eh? Good enough to enter in the Show I reckon.

PEARL: We goin'…

ANNIE: Going. With a 'g'.

PEARL: Are we going to the Show?

ANNIE: Of course we are. Everyone goes to the Show.

PEARL: Whoppee! Can we see the Siamese twins and the bearded lady?

ANNIE: If you're good.

PEARL: I'm always good.

ANNIE: That right?

PEARL: Uh-huh. See? I can go to bed without being told.

ANNIE: Go on then.

    *She jumps up. The medal rolls onto the ground.*

  Hey!

PEARL: What?

ANNIE: Don't play innocent with me.

PEARL: What, Mum?

ANNIE: You been playing that two-up again, haven't you?

PEARL: No…

ANNIE: With this? I ought to give you a hiding. This' a medal. Your grandad won this in the war. It's not a toy.

PEARL: Sorry.

ANNIE: So you should be. You ought to respect things like this.

PEARL: Yes, Mum.

ANNIE: Don't you start telling me fibs. You hear?

PEARL: Yes, Mum.

ANNIE: I won't stand for it. Now get into bed.

PEARL: 'Night, Mum…

ANNIE: You want to go to the Show? You do your homework.

> ANNIE *blows out the light. There is a noise outside. In the darkness* ANNIE *grabs a sugar bag and signals to* PEARL *who climbs into it.* ANNIE *secures the bag tightly and throws some clothing on top of it. This is a well-rehearsed routine.*

Don't make a sound.

> *Scratching at the window. A face appears.* ANNIE *grabs something to defend herself.*

Sssh.

> ANNIE *hides as a* MAN *climbs in the window. He shines a torch.*

MAN: Anyone home?

> *The torch finds* ANNIE.

ANNIE: You stay…

> PAT *laughs and shines the torch on his own face.*

PAT: Got ya, eh?

ANNIE: Pat?

PAT: How ya goin, sis?

ANNIE: Bugger me dead, Pat, you nearly gave me a heart attack.

> *She hugs and punches him at the same time.*

PAT: Where's me little girl?

ANNIE: Crikey! What are you...? The Show... of course!

PAT: Told you I'd drop in.

ANNIE: Yeah, it's only been a year.

PAT: It's not—

ANNIE: Yes it is.

>     PEARL *emerges from the sugar bag.*

PEARL: Uncle Pat!

PAT: Look at you.

ANNIE: Grown, eh?

PAT: Big girl now.

PEARL: Guess what?

PAT: What?

PEARL: I've been real... really good too... haven't I, Mum?

ANNIE: Pull the other one.

PEARL: I have!

PAT: Oh dear! Shame you haven't been good...

PEARL: Aw... Mum! I've tried...

PAT: Yeah? Has she, sis?

ANNIE: Well... she's been... okay... I suppose.

PAT: I dunno, if she hasn't been good...

ANNIE: She's been all right.

>     PAT *leans out the window and pulls in a hessian bag.* PEARL *is beside herself. The sound of a dog (Rusty) barking.*

What you got in there?

PAT: Thought you might be in need of a feed. Lie down, Rusty! Lie down!

>     *The dog stops barking. He holds up the bag.*

Look what I found!

ANNIE: Found?

>     *He pulls out a plucked chook and holds it by the neck.*

PAT: Yeah. I was wandering along and all of a sudden this big, fat chook jumped into me bag here. What was I to do? Couldn't leave it there, could I?

ANNIE: Pat...

PAT: Thought it was Christmas.

ANNIE: You'll get caught one of these days.

PAT: No one's quick enough to catch me, sis.

ANNIE: Why take the risk, it's not as if we're starving…

PAT: Don't you like chook?

PEARL: I love chook.

ANNIE: Into bed with you.

PEARL: Aw…

PAT: Oh! Crikey! I nearly forgot.

PEARL: What?

PAT: Look what else I found.

> *He gives her a bright, red apple.* PEARL *tries to disguise her disappointment.*

PEARL: Oh, thanks, Uncle Pat.

ANNIE: Where'd that come from?

PAT: Eh?

ANNIE: Pinched it, didn't you?

PAT: That ol' Mission Manager'll never miss one apple.

ANNIE: You'll get us into strife…

PAT: And… seein' as I missed your birthday…

> *He takes a packet from his other pocket and gives it to* PEARL. *She unwraps it. It is a 1954 shilling commemorating the Coronation.*

That'll be worth a quid one day.

PEARL: A shilling!

PAT: It's not any old shilling! It was struck 'specially for the Queen's Coronation. You hang on to that.

PEARL: [*reading*] '1954'. Gee. It's old.

PAT: Yep.

PEARL: Now I got something to play two-up with!

ANNIE: Gawd!

> PEARL *spins it. Five times. Five heads!*

PEARL: Five heads in a row! Whatcha reckon?

ANNIE: You speak properly, girl.

PAT: Not bad. Back a tail next.

ANNIE: Do you mind?

PAT: What?

ANNIE: Teaching my girl bad habits!

PEARL: My lucky coin!

*She carefully puts it away.*

PAT: Oh… and there's these lollies.

PEARL: Thank you, Uncle Pat!

*She gives him a big hug and jumps into bed with her presents as* ANNIE *hides the chook.*

PAT: Good thing I remembered the lollies, eh?

ANNIE: You spoil her.

PAT: Nah!

ANNIE: Ratbag.

PAT: Who you callin' a ratbag?

ANNIE: You.

PAT: You oughta bloody talk.

ANNIE: Oi, you watch your language.

PAT: Oh, sorry.

ANNIE: The way you're going, we'll be eatin' like toffs soon.

PEARL: What's a toff?

ANNIE: You get to sleep.

PAT: A whitefella!

PEARL: Aren't there any blackfella toffs?

PAT: Not many, apart from me that is!

PEARL: What is it?

PAT: 'A fellow that is distinguished and walks like this.'

ANNIE: And drinks like this.

*She demonstrates. They continue, a little performance.*

PAT: And bows like this.

ANNIE: And curtsies like this.

PAT: A gentleman who wears nice clothes and escorts his lady in a proper way. 'Madam'.

ANNIE: 'Sir'.

*They waltz around the room humming 'The Blue Danube'.*

PEARL: Bravo!

ANNIE: Whoo…

PAT: You're knocked up there, sis! Need a bit o' track work I reckon!

ANNIE: Very funny.

PAT: You never know what might be around the corner!

ANNIE: Don't be silly.

PAT: There'll be some young fella…

ANNIE: Sshh…

*She points to* PEARL.

PAT: Well?

ANNIE: [*whispering*] Don't tell anyone.

PAT: 'Course not.

ANNIE *leads him away to where* PEARL *can't hear.*

ANNIE: There is a… a… bloke…

PAT: Blackfella?

ANNIE: Yeah! He's an abalone diver.

PAT: Oh.

ANNIE: We're just friends…

PAT: 'Course!

ANNIE: [*indicating* PEARL] Till she's a bit older.

PAT: Uh-huh.

ANNIE: Gotta see her right first.

PAT: Sure.

ANNIE *turns to find* PEARL *straining to listen.*

ANNIE: I'll give you the stick!

PEARL *hides under the blanket.* ANNIE *turns back to* PAT.

Unless you stayed around to give me a hand.

PAT: Eh?

ANNIE: Wouldn't you like a bit of family life for a change? Plenty of work 'round here. One of the dairy farms…

PAT: Dairy farm? Milking cows! Pull the other one!

ANNIE: What about fishing?

PAT: Thought I might head up north for a bit.

ANNIE: Oh.

PAT: Yeah. Bloody cold in the Highlands.

ANNIE: How far?

PAT: North Queensland. Maybe further west into the Gulf Country. Who knows?

ANNIE: We'll never see you.

PAT: 'Course you will… I'll be back in a few months.

ANNIE: Yeah?

PAT: Here, got something for you…

*He hands her some money.*

Tide you over while I'm away.

ANNIE: Hell's bells, Pat.

PAT: What's the matter?

ANNIE: Where'd this come from?

PAT: Where'd you reckon?

ANNIE: Pinching a chook is one thing but…

PAT: You reckon I pinched this, do you?

ANNIE: Well?

PAT: I earnt it.

ANNIE: Earnt it? Pull the other one.

PAT: I did.

ANNIE: Who's gonna pay you this sort of money?

*As* PAT *tells his yarn* PEARL *sits up and listens.*

PAT: This fella I was working for, his son is a bit of a lad. Known to go off the rails from time to time. Anyway, one night we were sitting 'round the fire playin' a bit of poker and I was startin' to hit a bit of a purple patch. Started cleanin' everyone out. In the end it was only me and the young bloke left. Well, he reckoned he had a pretty good hand so he put the lot on it. I reckoned I could match him so I raised him, but he was broke. He couldn't see me unless he could raise the extra cash. Poor bugger was desperate. One of those fellas whose eyes go all weird when they're having a bet.

It didn't matter much to me so I let him see me even though he didn't have the cash. He promised he'd settle no matter what. 'Sure', I thought, 'He won't pay up'. But I didn't care. It was only money. So. I laid out me cards. Royal Flush! The young bloke nearly died. He had a Full House and he still couldn't beat me. Off he went into the night cursin' and kickin' everything in sight. I got into me sleeping bag thinkin' it'd be the last I'd hear of it. 'Course I never expected him to pay up. He was the boss's son after all. Well, blow me down if a few hours later up he stumbles, full as a boot, and slings a wad of notes at me. 'Don't tell father!' And off he goes leavin' me lying there covered in quid notes. Just shows you, you never know what's…

PEARL: … waiting around the corner.

ANNIE: Will you go to sleep?

PAT: You remember that, bub.

ANNIE: I can't take your money.

PAT: Save it for a rainy day. Go on. Plenty more where that came from.

ANNIE: I suppose I could get her a new school uniform.

PEARL: A fishing line?

ANNIE: Or that book of poems.

PEARL: Poems?

PAT: Get yourselves an outfit. You'll be the best-lookin' sorts at the Show!

◆ ◆ ◆ ◆ ◆

## SCENE FIVE

*1963. The Show.*

JOE *prepares for the woodchop.*

P.A.: [*voice-over*] Here he is. Joe Turner. Last year's champ. The best axeman this district's seen for a many a year. Step up, Joe, and take a bow. Come on, folks! Give the local lad a cheer. That's the way. Now where's his opponent? Running late? Gone walkabout? No, only joking, here he is.

PAT *steps forward.*

The challenger from out of town… what's his name? Dodd. The boy Dodd. Righto, boys, pick up your axes. Are you ready?

*A bell rings.*

And away they go. Flat chat. Neck and neck, the chips are flying! Joe's got the best of it but the darkie's coming back at him. Go, Joe! Come on, son. This' a ring-dinger of a contest! A real nail biter. It's blow for blow as they fight it out, but look out! By jingoes! Young Dodd's inching in front. He's going like the clappers. He can wield an axe, this lad. Come on, Joe, put your back into it! Hooley dooley, the boy Dodd's got the money. What a display! They'll be celebrating down the blackfellas camp tonight. Bad luck, Joe. Collect your prize money behind the grandstand, boys.

PAT *and* JOE *shake hands.*

PAT: Jeez, you made me work for it.

JOE: Bloody axe. Knew I shoulda used the other one.

PAT: Thanks.

JOE: Yeah, thanks. Don't know what happened.

PAT: I musta got lucky.

JOE: You're pretty handy with that thing.

PAT: Reckon?

JOE: If you hadn't showed up I'd have been home and hosed.

PAT: Sorry about that.

JOE: Next time. Didn't think you were a timber man, knew your old man was, but…

PAT: Must be in the blood.

JOE: Yeah.

PAT: Prefer animals. 'Specially horses.

JOE: Know what you mean. That's why I'm working out the Mission now. That sleeper cutting's too bloody hard.

PAT: You're workin' out the Mission?

JOE: Yeah.

PAT: Seen me sister?

JOE: Who?

PAT: Annie. You know…

JOE: Nah… haven't seen her 'round.

PAT: You know who she is though.

JOE: Yeah.

PAT: Tell you what…

JOE: Eh?

PAT: I'll do you a deal. You look out for her and the girl and I'll give you my share of the prize money.

JOE: You're joking?

PAT: Fair dink.

JOE: All of it?

PAT: The lot.

JOE: Jeez.

PAT: Don't you tell Annie though. She's not to know. Just keep an eye on them for me, all right?

JOE: I dunno…

PAT: You look out for them and you'll do all right for yourself.

JOE: How?

PAT: There'll be a bonus for you every time I come home. Good money.

JOE: What'd you mean?

PAT: I'm goin' bush. Takin' off now. Goin' drovin'. She... me sis... she don't want me to go, but... I've got to keep movin'.

JOE: You in trouble?

PAT: Nuh. Just... gotta keep movin'. I need someone to watch over them though. Can you do it?

JOE: Righto.

PAT: Sure?

JOE: I'll do me best.

PAT: See? Giving you a hand with that axle that time done us both the power of good, eh?

JOE: 'Spose.

PAT: I hear that Manager's a bit of an old bastard.

JOE: When he's on the grog he is.

PAT: Make sure he leaves her alone.

JOE: I can handle him.

PAT: It's a deal?

JOE: Deal.

     *They shake.*

PAT: Don't let me down.

JOE: Crikey, the way you swing that thing, as if I'd let you down.

PAT: Good man.

JOE: Your shout.

PAT: Righto then...

◆ ◆ ◆ ◆ ◆

*SCENE SIX*

*1963. The Mission.*

ANNIE *and* PEARL *are in their new dresses.* PEARL *goes through her showbag.*

ANNIE: Ohh, my feet. You take a bit of keeping up to, my girl!

PEARL: It was fun. 'Specially when Uncle Pat won the woodchop.

ANNIE: He likes to win!

PEARL: Why can't he stay here for a while?

ANNIE: He's one of those men who just can't stay in the one place or stick to the one thing. He's a Jack of All Trades. He can live anywhere and do anything.

PEARL: I wish he'd live here.

ANNIE: Me too.

PEARL: When will we see him again?

ANNIE: I don't know, it's like... Hop into bed and I'll tell you a story.

PEARL *hops into bed.*

You could take your dress off.

PEARL: Can't I sleep in it tonight? Please?

ANNIE: Oh, all right. Just this once.

PEARL: Go on.

ANNIE: Well, you know how Uncle Pat breaks horses?

PEARL: Yeah.

ANNIE: How the horse turns out might depend on its master. If its master is kind and gentle and doesn't pull too tightly on the bit then the horse will grow up strong and confident and still be prancing around no matter what happens. If the master's mean the horse has to learn very quickly to do whatever its master wants or it'll get thrashed. Probably get thrashed anyway. If it's lucky it'll end up like an old draught horse, just plodding along minding its own business, keeping out of trouble.

Other horses are so badly broken in that all the thrashings break their spirit and they just give up. Then there's the ones like Uncle Pat. They never lose their fight, no matter what. If they're lucky they end up in the rodeo. If not they're whipped and beaten until they're black and blue because they just won't be broken. They buck and kick and bite and refuse to be harnessed. They're like wild brumbies. Sadly they're never allowed to run around a paddock or eat good hay. They end up fighting all the way to the end. They don't trust anyone so, even if someone is being good to them, they're so angry they just keep on lashing out. They're the ones that often end up in the knackery.

PEARL: I hope Uncle Pat doesn't end up in the knackery!

ANNIE: Fat chance. They couldn't break him at the Boys' Home. Gave him more thrashings than you've had hot dinners, but he wouldn't be broken. He never will. I suppose that's why he's always on the move. No paddock can hold him, eh? Now go on, off to sleep.

PEARL: Love you, Mum.

ANNIE: You too.

> *She blows out the candle and begins to undress. A scratch at the window.*

Pat?

PEARL: He hasn't gone yet!

> *More scratching. She re-lights the candle.*

ANNIE: Right-oh!

> *A man climbs in. It is* JOE. *He grabs her.*

JOE: Sshh!

ANNIE: Wha—?!

JOE: Quiet!

> *The sound of a truck. Doors slam.*

Listen.

> *He covers her mouth.*

Listen!

> *She breaks free.*

ANNIE: What do you think you're doing?

JOE: Hear that?

> *Voices.*

ANNIE: Yes?

JOE: Protection Board.

> ANNIE *grabs* PEARL.

ANNIE: No!

JOE: District Welfare Officer reckons you lot aren't lookin' after your kids.

ANNIE: Me?

JOE: None of you.

ANNIE: Oh, God!

JOE: Get her dressed. Come on, Annie, get cracking.

PEARL: What is it, Mum?

JOE: Quick, girlie, hop to it.

PEARL: Mum?

JOE: For Christ's sake, Annie, get a wriggle on, will you?

ANNIE: Here. Don't let them take her, Joe…

JOE: Quiet, Annie.

PEARL: Take me? Who—?

JOE: Now listen carefully, girl. I want you to climb out the window
   …

ANNIE: What?

JOE: Shut up! Okay, you know Donny Carter?

PEARL: Who?

JOE: The rabbit man, with the red hair.

PEARL: Oh, yeah—

JOE: Good-oh. Donny's waiting outside and he's gonna look after you
   for a while.

ANNIE: Hang on.

JOE: I'm tellin' you, Annie, you're gonna have to trust me. Donny's
   gonna take her to his place till they go. Tell her to do as I say. Go
   on, tell her.

   *The sounds of parents screaming, babies crying.*

   Christ! Come on…

ANNIE: Listen, bubby—

JOE: The rabbit man's gonna take you to his place and hide you there.

   *Torch lights flashing.*

   They won't be lookin' around his place.

ANNIE: Understand?

PEARL: Yes, Mum.

   *A torch shines through the window.*

JOE: Get down!

   *He forces them onto the floor.* ANNIE *grabs* PEARL.

   Make sure she does exactly as I say, Annie.

ANNIE: Do as Joe says.

PEARL: Yes, Mum.

JOE: Hop out the window and be as quiet as you can.

ANNIE: Go on.

> *Footsteps approach. A knock.*

JOE: Hold on!

> *He grabs her and pushes her towards the window.*

Get going.

VOICE: [*offstage*] Open up!

> JOE *bundles* PEARL *out the window. He grabs* ANNIE *and throws her on the floor.*

JOE: Do as I say…

> *The torch shines through another window.*

Groan.

ANNIE: What?

JOE: Groan, like you're enjoyin' yourself.

> *The torch arcs through the window like a spotlight searching for a rabbit.*

ANNIE: Ohh… ohhh…

JOE: That's it! More…

ANNIE: Ohh…

JOE: Say you like it.

ANNIE: What?

JOE: Go on…

ANNIE: Ohh… ohh… that's… that's good…

JOE: Yeah, yeah…

VOICE: [*offstage*] What's going on in there?

JOE: More!

ANNIE: What?

JOE: More noise…

ANNIE: Ahhh… ohh… yes… yes… yes…

VOICE: [*offstage*] Oi!

> *He rips at* ANNIE*'s top, tearing it off her, then springs to his feet. The light finds him.*

JOE: [*calling out*] For Christ's sake… hang on! [*He lights a lantern and takes a swig of scotch from a hip flask. Calling again*] What's goin' on? [*To* ANNIE] Laugh! Go on. Pretend you're enjoying yourself.

> ANNIE *follows his instructions.* JOE *tosses the hip flask onto the bed and undoes his belt, dropping his trousers as he hobbles over to the door.*

Can't you give a bloke a bit of peace…?

> *He opens the door. The torch hits his eyes.*

VOICE: [*offstage*] Oh, shit! Sorry, Joe.

JOE: Yeah? What do you want?

> *The torch shines on* ANNIE.

Not bad, eh?

> *The torch searches the room.*

Sorry, fellas, you caught me at a bad time…

ANNIE: You comin' back to bed?

JOE: Likes it, this one. Can I help you?

VOICE: [*offstage*] Where's the lass?

JOE: There.

VOICE: [*offstage*] The young'un.

JOE: Dunno what you're talking about. This one, she's on her own, aren't you, love?

ANNIE: Yes, Boss.

VOICE: [*offstage*] Must have the wrong address. Sorry, mate. Owe you a beer.

> *Doors slam and the truck moves off to the next house. The sound of it stopping, doors, voices.*

ANNIE: Bastards!

> *Mayhem outside.*

The others…

JOE: You can't worry about them.

ANNIE: I gotta do something, warn them…

JOE: Settle down.

ANNIE: I can't…

JOE: You stop here or you'll lose the girl.

*More sound of screaming, crying, doors slamming. Babies being taken away.*

Sssh. Don't draw attention…

ANNIE: What about my baby?

JOE: She'll be all right. Donny owes me a favour.

ANNIE: Dear God…

JOE: Here. Have a swig.

ANNIE: I don't drink.

JOE: Sorry I frightened you like that.

ANNIE: Don't worry about it. Thanks, Joe. I really mean that, thanks a lot.

JOE: No worries.

ANNIE: Pearl'll be scared stiff.

JOE: Calm down. Donny's missus'll look after her. Here. Relax. Take it easy, will you?

ANNIE: You reckon they believed you?

JOE: Welfare always listen to me, Annie.

ANNIE: Will they be back?

JOE: Maybe.

ANNIE: Won't they report you?

JOE: Me? What for? It's all under control. Go on, have a drink?

ANNIE: No thanks.

JOE: You could save yourself a lot of trouble you know.

ANNIE: How?

JOE: Get yourself an Exemption Certificate.

ANNIE: A 'Dog Licence'?

JOE: All you have to do is move off the Mission. Set yourself up in town. I often have a beer with the District Welfare Officer, be no problem to put in a good word for you. They look favourably on blackfellas who do the right thing.

ANNIE: These are my people. I don't want to move away from them.

JOE: Government wants to get rid of places like this.

ANNIE: Missions?

JOE: Uh-huh. Assim… assimi… here… [*He pulls a piece of paper out of his back pocket and tries to read it.*] 'Policy of Assimm…' Oh, bugger it! What's this word?

ANNIE: Assim-il-a-tion. What's that?

JOE: Buggered if I know, but they want youse to move off here that's all I know.

> *Silence. Outside the noise has died down. The sound of sobbing can be heard.*

ANNIE: I'll be all right, you can go now, thanks…

JOE: I better stay for a while, eh? Just in case.

ANNIE: They won't bother me now.

JOE: Reckon one good turn deserves another. What do you think?

ANNIE: What?

JOE: You know.

ANNIE: No?

JOE: Relax, Annie. Come and sit here.

ANNIE: Why?

JOE: Why do you think?

ANNIE: Oh, come on, Joe…

JOE: [*approaching her*] I've always liked you, Annie, you know that.

ANNIE: Don't be silly…

JOE: You're real pretty, Annie.

ANNIE: Please go.

JOE: Why?

ANNIE: Because I want you to.

JOE: You want to lose your girl or keep her? One word from me…

ANNIE: You wouldn't…

JOE: 'One good turn…'

ANNIE: Joe…

JOE: Don't you like me?

ANNIE: Don't…

JOE: I want to look after you. You do the right thing by me…

ANNIE: What do you mean?

JOE: I could take good care of you. You move into town, I could… you know…

ANNIE: I'm not moving.

JOE: I like you a lot, Annie.

ANNIE: Now look…

JOE: I like you a real lot.

ANNIE: I'm sorry…

JOE: I could look after you and the girl. We could, you know, make a go of it...

ANNIE: Stop, Joe.

JOE: This is your big chance, Annie. I... I'm not real good at this sort of thing. You know what I'm askin', don't you? I'm asking you to be my girl.

ANNIE: Oh no...

JOE: I'll...

ANNIE: I can't ...

JOE: Why?

ANNIE: Because... I'm sorry but... thanks for asking but...

JOE: You knockin' me back? Are you?

ANNIE: I just don't feel like that about you, that's all.

JOE: You don't want me to call them back, do you? Eh? They'll be in town for a few hours yet. Roundin' up stray kids. You know the Protection Board. They're not proud. Room enough in their truck for that girl of yours I reckon.

ANNIE: Please, Joe...

JOE: I mean, I went to a bit of trouble on your behalf. I reckon you could say thank you, don't you? Mmm?

ANNIE: I did.

JOE: Now come on...

*He approaches her lasciviously.*

ANNIE: Hey...

JOE: Don't be scared...

ANNIE: What are you—?

JOE: I know you like me.

ANNIE: I don't... not like that...

JOE: You're makin' me feel real randy, you know that?

ANNIE: No, no...

JOE: Jeez, you look sexy...

ANNIE: Don't...

JOE: Come here.

*He grabs her and forces a kiss on her.*

Christ, you smell good.

ANNIE: No...

JOE: Feel that.

> *He grabs her hand and puts it on his crutch.*

That's how you make me feel.

ANNIE: Get away!

JOE: Ohh, Jesus… I'm been dreaming about doing this… You've got the best tits… Ohhh… I've spent a lot of nights thinkin' about you…

ANNIE: You can't…

JOE: I'm not going to hurt you, girl. I'll be real gentle. Just lie still. Go on. Let me feel you, Annie, let me… Don't fight it, baby…

> ANNIE *momentarily gives in to him. Just as he lets go of her she pushes him away and goes to where she hid the money* PAT *gave her.*

What are you doing?

ANNIE: Here. Please. Take it.

JOE: Where'd this come from?

ANNIE: I… I got it.

JOE: How?

ANNIE: Saved it. It's for Pearl. To go to school.

JOE: You been up to no good, girl? You been stealin'?

ANNIE: No. 'Course not. You know me.

JOE: Could be trouble.

ANNIE: Please take it.

JOE: You sure?

ANNIE: Please.

> *He pockets the money.*

JOE: You haven't been on the game, have you?

ANNIE: Piss off!

JOE: Ahhh, Jesus, Annie…

ANNIE: Get out of here, Joe, you got my savings…

JOE: Where's someone like you going to get this sort of money then, eh?

ANNIE: Pat.

JOE: Your brother? What's he, the bloody paymaster around here?

ANNIE: What?

JOE: Now look… Welfare's lookin' for your daughter, your brother's pissed off… you've just given me a bribe… I reckon you oughta come here and pay me back or else… I'll have to get on the blower.

*He chases her around the room and finally grabs her.*

ANNIE: Get away from me!

JOE: You want it, don't you?

ANNIE: You're disgusting.

JOE: All this talk about sex n'stuff… drive a bloke mad…

*He forces his crutch against her. She tries to pull away.*

ANNIE: Let go…!

JOE: Ohh… that feels good, doesn't it?

*She struggles.*

Doesn't that feel good?

*She hits him.*

Oh… right…

ANNIE: No…

JOE: You don't know what's good for you, woman.

*He grabs her. They fight. He overpowers her.*

ANNIE: Don't!

JOE: How's it feel, eh?

ANNIE: Get away!

JOE: Heard about you black gins. Pretty wild, eh? Jeez, you're a strong little—

ANNIE: Get off me—!

*She bites him.*

JOE: Come on, Annie! Ow! Fightin's one thing but bitin'…

ANNIE: Please…

JOE: You little bitch! That's the thanks I get, is it?

ANNIE: Don't, Joe, please don't…

JOE: Like a bit of stick, eh? Is that what you like? You're a goer, all right… here…

*He hits her and forces himself onto her. Her screams are echoed by the screams outside.*

Scream away! No one'll know the difference. I knew you wanted it... Doesn't that feel good? Feel that! Yeah. You black cunt... you beautiful black cunt.

◆ ◆ ◆ ◆ ◆

*SCENE SEVEN*

*1963. A country courtroom.*

PAT *stands in front of a magistrate.*

PAT: Beg your pardon, Your Honour. I know what you might think, like, I know I've been in a bit of strife before, but... I'm real sorry. I am. I never meant to, you know... get involved... but... the truth is... I had no choice. You see, Your Honour, the thing is, I'm not a violent sort of a bloke. I'm like me dad. I only fight when I have to. But the thing is, what would you expect a bloke to do? I mean, I was minding me own business. I wasn't lookin' for strife. It's not true what that fella there said. I was just polishing me saddle and minding me own business. Then I heard this helluva racket. I jumped up to see what was goin' on.

He was lightin' into this dumb horse, giving it a terrible hiding, thrashing it with a bridle he was. Well. Just think what sort of damage that'd do with the bit and everything. So, I sung out to him, 'What do you think you're doing?' He took no notice of me, just kept on belting into it. You shoulda seen it, Your Honour, blood was pouring out of its mouth, big welts across its flanks. He woulda killed it, there's no doubt about that. I had to do something. In the end I just sung out, 'You drop that bridle or I'll drop you!'

As he turned around the horse reared up and he lost his grip. It took off. Then he starts abusing me, calling me names and stuff. I told him he could call me what he liked but that was no way to treat a dumb animal. That's what my dad always said to me, you see. 'Never be cruel to dumb animals. A man can fight back but a dumb animal's got no chance.' Anyway, the horse had bolted, so I told him I hoped he'd learnt a bloody good lesson!

I left him to it but, then, before I'd gone a few paces, I felt this whack across the back of me head. Jeez, it hurt! That bloody mongrel there had belted me with the bridle. What did he think I was? A dumb animal? Not bloody likely. Sorry 'bout that, I know you shouldn't swear, but I got a bit carried away. The thing is, Your Honour, I can go a bit and, you know, well, a bloke king-hits you. What are you meant to do? Anyway, before I knew it he was down for the count. No wonder he only attacked dumb animals. He couldn't fight his way out of a paper bag! Gutless wonder!

That's it, Your Honour. How was I to know he was the Shire President?

*The sound of the magistrate's gavel falling.*

❖ ❖ ❖ ❖ ❖

## SCENE EIGHT

*1966. A schoolyard.*

PEARL *is playing 'knuckles'. She is dressed in a Catholic primary school uniform. She lays four knuckles on the ground. She picks one up and throws it in the air, then picks up another and catches it in the same hand. She tosses the two into the air and picks up a third. She throws three in the air and tries to catch a fourth. She sings to herself—a song from the period.* NELL, *a young nun, enters.*

NELL: What are you doing out here all by yourself?
PEARL: Playing.
NELL: Where are your shoes?
PEARL: In my bag.
NELL: You better put them on.
PEARL: Do you want to have a go?

*She offers* NELL *the knuckles.*

NELL: Put your shoes on.
PEARL: Aw, Sister…
NELL: Go on. You are meant to be a young lady.

PEARL *puts on her shoes as* NELL *tosses the knuckles from hand to hand.*

I used to play knuckles as a girl.

PEARL: Did you?

NELL: It's a very old game.

PEARL: Must be! Sorry, Sister, only joking.

NELL: They used to use sheep's knuckles.

PEARL: Real sheep?

NELL: That's what my dad told me.

PEARL: My dad used to steal sheep.

NELL: Oh…

PEARL: He got put in jail for stealing sheep.

NELL: That's terrible.

PEARL: He was a swaggie.

NELL: Really?

PEARL: Yeah, jumped into a billabong…

NELL: Did he?

PEARL: 'And his ghost may be heard…'

NELL: You little… you mustn't tell fibs.

PEARL: Sorry, Sister!

NELL: Scallywag.

> *A ball hits* PEARL *in the middle of the back. Offstage giggles. She picks it up and pegs it in the direction of the giggles.*

[*Calling*] Who threw—?

PEARL: Don't worry, Sister.

NELL: [*calling*] Girls!

PEARL: Please. It doesn't matter.

NELL: They've disappeared.

PEARL: Have a go.

> PEARL *offers her the knuckles as* NELL *searches for the culprits.*

NELL: Do you know who they are?

PEARL: Nuh. Here…

NELL: If I find out…

PEARL: Forget it.

> NELL *tries to play knuckles. Her attempts are unsuccessful.* PEARL *laughs.*

You need to practise.

NELL: I do.

> PEARL *takes them off her and plays throughout the scene.*

You're very good at that. Maybe if you put as much effort into your reading as you do games, you might get better grades.

PEARL: Yes, Sister.

NELL: I found you a poem for the recital. Elizabeth Hardwicke. Hope you like it.

> *She gives* PEARL *a book of poetry.*

PEARL: Thanks. Do you like it here?

NELL: Yes. So far.

PEARL: Where did you come from?

NELL: The city.

PEARL: Thought so. Whereabouts?

NELL: Sydney.

PEARL: Gawd!

NELL: Long way away.

PEARL: What's it like?

NELL: It's very beautiful. It's like here, near the sea. Our convent overlooked the city on one side and the ocean on the other.

PEARL: I've never been to the city.

NELL: You will one day.

PEARL: You're like me.

NELL: Oh?

PEARL: You don't fit in.

NELL: Thanks!

PEARL: You're too young to be a nun.

NELL: Really?

PEARL: Yeah. And too pretty.

NELL: Thank you.

PEARL: The other nuns are…

NELL: Now, now.

PEARL: They look like witches.

NELL: Pearl!

PEARL: You don't want to look like a witch, do you?

NELL: No.

PEARL: Why'd you become a nun?

NELL: What sort of a question is that?

PEARL: Well?

NELL: You ask a lot of questions.

PEARL: Did God call you?

*The bell rings.*

NELL: Someone's calling you!

PEARL: Did He?

NELL: Yes. I suppose He did. In a way.

PEARL: Did you always want to be a nun?

NELL: Pearl, the bell's gone.

PEARL: Worse luck…

NELL: Hurry up. You'll get into trouble.

PEARL: Do you a deal.

NELL: Come on!

PEARL: Tell me why you became a nun and I'll show you 'round.

NELL: What?

PEARL: Lots of things 'round here only us mob know about.

NELL: Will you?

PEARL: Yeah, someone's got to.

NELL: Why's that?

PEARL: You haven't got many friends.

NELL: You're incorrigible. Now get a move on!

PEARL: Deal?

PEARL *runs off.*

NELL: All right, deal! Don't forget your homework!

*She sees the poetry book which* PEARL *has left behind.*

Pearl! Your poetry… Dear God, what am I going to do with her?

◆ ◆ ◆ ◆ ◆

## SCENE NINE

*1966.*

PEARL *skips with a skipping rope as she recites her poem.*[1]

---

[1] Elizabeth Hardwicke, 'Our Babies' from *Numbers from the Old Land and New*, 1894.

PEARL: 'Twas a darling little baby,
    And she prattled, oh, so sweet,
    As she toddled up the roadway
    On her tiny, fairy feet.

    In my arms I clasped her closely,
    And pressed kisses on her cheek—
    Kissed cheek, and lip and forehead,
    But a word I could not speak;

    For my heart was filled with longing
    For my babies of long ago,
    And troubled thoughts came thronging
    That our lives should alter so;

    For my babies all have vanish'd—
    Changed to men and women grown,
    And I love them: still I'm famished
    For the baby love that's flown.

    Gone, ah! where I cannot tell you,
    But I miss it every day;
    And I'm fain to kiss sweet toddlers
    That may meet me by the way.

◆ ◆ ◆ ◆ ◆

*SCENE TEN*

*A few weeks later. The Mission.*

JOE *is getting dressed.* ANNIE *huddles under the bedclothes.*

JOE: Sent me report in. I can't keep bullshittin' forever. They're gonna find out sooner or later. Dunno why you don't take up me offer. I'll look after you. You could do a lot worse, you know.

    *He tries to kiss her. She pulls away.*

    Jeez, you're a cranky bloody thing. Why don't you just wake up to yourself and make it easier for all of us? What do you want? I'm offerin' to marry you. You know what Welfare thinks about kids being raised without a proper family. Pearl needs lookin' after. Don't be so bloody ungrateful. That's your trouble, Annie, you're too bloody proud.

*A knock on the door.* ANNIE *jumps up and gets dressed.*

Shit! Who's that?

ANNIE: Pat?

*Another knock.*

NELL: [*offstage*] Hello!

JOE: Answer her.

ANNIE: Yes?

NELL: [*offstage*] Mrs Dodd?

ANNIE: Yes.

NELL: [*offstage*] It's Sister Roberts from Pearl's school.

JOE: Shit!

ANNIE: Hang on a sec.

JOE: Go on, let her in. Hey! Don't forget the Protection Board are due next week.

ANNIE *lets* NELL *in.*

NELL: How do you do, Mrs Dodd.

*She offers her hand. They shake.*

Mr Dodd…

JOE: Eh? Yeah… g'day… I mean… ah… how do you do.

JOE *shakes her hand.*

NELL: I hope you don't mind…

ANNIE: Mind?

NELL: … me calling around… I didn't know how to contact you…

JOE: I better be off then. Work… you know…

*He sidles out as* ANNIE *rushes around tidying up.*

ANNIE: Sorry about the mess.

NELL: Please, don't bother.

ANNIE: I've been flat out. Normally it's much tidier. I keep it clean.

NELL: Of course.

ANNIE: I've been bottling plums. To sell. Bit of extra for Pearl's books and…

NELL: Mrs Dodd, I'm not here to inspect…

ANNIE: Oh no. I know. Please sit down. It's not very comfortable but…

NELL: It's fine. You should see my room!

ANNIE: It'd be spotless I bet!

NELL: Well, yes it is. Although I have to admit it's not entirely because of me.

ANNIE: Oh?

NELL: Mother Superior.

ANNIE: Oh, yes…

NELL: I'd be in big trouble if… if everything wasn't one hundred percent. Hospital corners, no creases. Got to pass inspection!

    *Silence.*

ANNIE: Oh. Sorry. Cuppa?

NELL: Um… Oh, yes. Please.

ANNIE: How'd you have it? Black?!

NELL: White and two…

ANNIE: 'Course.

    NELL *pulls a book out of her bag.*

NELL: I brought this.

ANNIE: Lord Byron? Who's he when he's at home?

NELL: I thought Pearl might like it. English romantic.

ANNIE: Oh.

NELL: She seems to like poetry.

ANNIE: Isn't she a bit young…?

NELL: A classical education will stand her in good stead.

ANNIE: Right. I'll make sure she reads it then. Sit down. Go on.

NELL: Thank you. Actually that's what I came about. Pearl's reading.

ANNIE: What's wrong with it?

NELL: Nothing's wrong at all. It's just that she is particularly bright and I think she would be well served by some coaching.

ANNIE: Coaching?

NELL: Yes.

ANNIE: I can't afford coaching.

NELL: I'd be happy to help.

ANNIE: She hasn't got time.

NELL: Pearl's got enormous potential.

ANNIE: She's passing her tests, isn't she?

NELL: Yes, but she could do so much better.

ANNIE: I'll make her read more. As long as she finishes her chores. I can't do everything on my own. I need her to help me.

NELL: Of course…

ANNIE: She's never missed a day…

NELL: Please, Mrs Dodd. Pearl is a wonderful student.

ANNIE: She better be!

NELL: Have you… have you ever thought of sending her away?

ANNIE: Away?

NELL: To boarding school.

ANNIE: No.

NELL: She's so gifted, I'm sure she could win a scholarship. In fact…

*She presents* ANNIE *with forms.*

I took the liberty to make a few inquiries. Her academic record alone may not win her a scholarship but, combined with her sporting prowess…

ANNIE: You working for Welfare?

NELL: Welfare?

ANNIE: No one's taking my girl…

NELL: I just… it's… I mean she's so bright and talented. I thought… I wanted to help.

ANNIE: To help?

NELL: Yes. To help Pearl.

ANNIE: By sending her away?

NELL: Only to school. Lots of country children go to boarding school. Please consider it. I went to a school where there were boarders and they had a wonderful time. Pearl would fit in beautifully. To be honest, Mrs Dodd, she would have a much better chance than they give her here, although you mustn't tell anyone I said that!

ANNIE: She'll be right.

NELL: What about your husband? Maybe…

ANNIE: My husband?

NELL: Yes. What does he think?

ANNIE: I haven't… Oh… him? Did you think…? He's not my husband.

NELL: Oh.

ANNIE: He's the new Manager.

NELL: I see.

ANNIE: He was doing his rounds.

NELL: Right.

ANNIE: He was… checking on us… that we were all right. He used to work here. When the other fella left… got the boot… they promoted him.

NELL: Are you all right?

ANNIE: Yes.

NELL: Is there something…?

ANNIE: I'm quite all right, thank you!

> *A whistle blows. It's the kettle. It is resonant of the train whistle from Scene One.*

You tell me if Pearl plays up, won't you?

NELL: She's perfect.

ANNIE: Yeah?

NELL: Truly.

ANNIE: No one's perfect.

NELL: No, but…

ANNIE: I'll get the kettle.

NELL: Mrs Dodd. You must understand, I'd do anything for Pearl. Anything.

ANNIE: Maybe you could give her a lesson or two. I'll give you some plum jam.

NELL: That would be lovely.

ANNIE: Good. Ah… I haven't got any milk.

NELL: Black'll be fine.

ANNIE: Much better, you know!

◆ ◆ ◆ ◆ ◆

## SCENE ELEVEN

*1966. The Mission.*

PEARL *is doing her Latin homework whilst munching on an apple.*

PEARL: 'Amo. Amas. Amat.' I love. You love. He, she, it loves.

'Amamus. Amatis. Amant.' We love. You love. They love.

ANNIE *enters. She rushes to a bucket and throws up.*

Mum?

ANNIE: It's all right.

PEARL: Shouldn't you see someone? You've been throwing up for days now.

ANNIE: Finished your homework?

PEARL: I hate Latin.

ANNIE: Get on with it.

PEARL: 'Amo. Amas. Am—'

ANNIE: Where'd that come from?

PEARL: Oh… I… someone gave it to me. At school.

ANNIE: I catch you pinching apples I'll tan your hide.

*She clutches her stomach.* PEARL *rushes to her.*

PEARL: Mum!

ANNIE: What did I do to deserve this?

PEARL: What?

ANNIE: Sit down, girl.

PEARL: What's the matter?

ANNIE: Joe.

PEARL: Oh. Him!

ANNIE: He's… maybe I should… you see. This is very… you see I'm…

*There is a knock at the door.*

Oh, hell.

*Another knock.*

Hang on…

*The knock is insistent.*

VOICE: [*offstage*] Open up! It's Sergeant Rankin.

ANNIE: Who?

VOICE: [*offstage*] Sergeant Rankin.

ANNIE *ushers* PEARL *to the window.*

ANNIE: Get goin'…

*'Sergeant Rankin' bursts in. It's* PAT, *his hat covering his face. He wears a suit. He puts on a voice.*

PAT: You been up to no good I hear.

ANNIE: Not me.

PAT *tosses back his hat and swoops her up into his arms.*

PAT: Bloody good thing too!

ANNIE: Oh, God…!

PEARL: Uncle Pat!

PAT: G'day, sis, how ya goin'?

ANNIE: You bloody fool!

PAT: Lovely welcome, that is! Look at you!

PEARL *rushes to him.*

PEARL: You're back.

PAT: That's more like it!

*He twirls her around.* ANNIE *sits holding her stomach.*

She's grown.

ANNIE: Really?

PAT: My oath.

ANNIE: They tend to.

PAT: Shut your eyes. [*He pulls a stockwhip out of his bag.*] Open!

PEARL: Wow!

PAT: Hand made.

PEARL: It's beautiful.

PAT: Here. I'll show you how to crack it.

*He demonstrates.*

ANNIE: Look out, you'll break something.

PAT: Not bad, eh?

PEARL: Can I have a go?

ANNIE: Not in here you can't.

PAT: You just flick it like this…

ANNIE: Pat!

PAT: Better take it outside and practise. I'll be out in a tic…

PEARL *exits with the whip.*

She's a good'un, eh?

ANNIE: At times…

PAT: So… Crikey! You look crook.

ANNIE: Thanks.

PAT: Didn't mean it like that, but… what's up?

ANNIE: Nothing. Bit of flu.

PAT: You look after yourself, you hear?

ANNIE: Shut up, Pat.

> *Silence.*

What's this then?

> *She points at his suit.*

PAT: Suits me, eh?

ANNIE: Pinch it, did you?

PAT: Off the hook!

ANNIE: I see.

PAT: I'm a respectable fella now.

ANNIE: That right?

PAT: True.

ANNIE: It's four years, bro…

PAT: Yeah. I know. I'm sorry…

ANNIE: Where you been?

PAT: Workin'…

ANNIE: Bullshit.

PAT: I have.

ANNIE: You going to tell me or not?

PAT: Nothin' to tell.

ANNIE: Get on with it!

> PAT *looks outside.*

PAT: Don't want her to know…

ANNIE: Bit late for that.

PAT: Shame job, eh?

ANNIE: Oh no, I'm sure you can talk your way out of it.

PAT: I'm sorry.

ANNIE: You're sorry! Get yourself tossed inside for fighting and God knows what else and you're sorry?

PAT: Wasn't my fault.

ANNIE: Never is.

> *The sound of the whip cracking.* PAT *indicates towards where* PEARL *is playing.*

PAT: Hey! One good thing. Learnt how to box in there. Properly. After I got out Jimmy Sharman took me on, then I had a few pro bouts up in WA and Queensland. Made a good quid too! Knocked out the Queensland Champion.

ANNIE: Bully for you.

PAT: Then I landed the Head Stockman's job? Out Alice Springs way. Dry out there, sis, and flat. Whoo. Flat. I seen some amazing things. I seen our people living in the desert. Like the old days. Learnt some language…

ANNIE: You said we'd stick together, Pat. Remember?

PAT: Yeah, I know, but…

ANNIE: That was the deal.

PAT: Hell, sis, I'm sorry, but you can't look a gift horse in the mouth, eh?

ANNIE: You let me down.

*The door flies open and in marches* JOE. *He carries the whip.*

JOE: What's she doing with a whip…? Oh… who's this? Oh, it's you. I thought…

ANNIE: They let him out.

PAT: G'day, Joe.

JOE: You got a permit?

PAT: What?

ANNIE: He's our Bossman now.

JOE: You know the score. You need a permit.

PAT: Calm down, Joe, I'm not gunna cause any strife.

JOE: They're the rules.

PAT: What's goin' on here?

JOE: Permit?

PAT: As a matter of fact…

*He hands* JOE *a piece of paper.*

There you go. Never thought I'd need it here!

JOE: Right. I'll check it with the coppers.

PAT: Suit yourself.

JOE: I don't want any trouble from you.

PAT: From me?

JOE: This doesn't concern you. It's about the girl.

PAT: I'm family.

JOE: She's trouble…

PEARL *appears in the doorway.* JOE *fishes a stone out of his pocket.*

Look what I found on me floor.

PAT: And?

JOE: Someone busted me window, didn't they?

PAT: Why would they do that?

ANNIE: Pat!

JOE: [*turning to* PEARL] Know anything?

PEARL: No.

JOE: Don't play innocent with me.

PEARL: I don't know what you're talking about.

JOE: Don't you just?

PEARL: No…

JOE: Bullshit you don't.

*He grabs* PEARL*'s arm.* PAT *takes a step forward.* ANNIE *stops him.*

[*Indicating the whip*] This yours?

PEARL: Nuh.

JOE: You're not as smart as you think, girlie.

PAT: Hey!

JOE: Something the matter?

PAT: Let her go.

JOE: Yeah?

PAT: Let her go!

ANNIE: Pat…

JOE: Aren't you on parole?

*He squeezes* PEARL*'s arm.*

PEARL: Ow!

JOE: You were seen near my place this arvo.

PEARL: I always walk past…

JOE: You know, I reckon I might just have to make a little phone call, I might.

ANNIE: No! Please… I promise it wasn't her.

PAT: How much?

JOE: Don't get smart—

PAT: How much was the window?

JOE: You keep out of it.

PAT: Reckon this should cover it?

*He fishes out a wad of notes.*

JOE: Where'd this come from?

PAT: Workin'.

JOE: For a... you always seem to have money, don't you?

PAT: Wouldn't complain if I were you.

JOE: Watch your step.

PAT: Sorry.

JOE: I don't want you causing trouble 'round here.

PAT: I'll be on me way now... 'Boss'!

JOE: Watch that smart mouth of yours, Pat.

PAT: Yes, 'Boss'.

JOE: I'm telling you, Annie. You better have a word to these two. You hear? This is your last chance. Understand?

ANNIE: Yes.

PAT: Fair enough, 'Boss'.

ANNIE: Pat!

PAT: Can I have me whip?

JOE: No you can't...

PAT *holds out his hand, a challenge.*

PAT: You got no rights over me, Joe. Just give it here.

JOE: [*wilting*] Take it with you.

PAT: No law 'gainst crackin' a whip, is there?

JOE: Don't forget, Annie. Last chance.

JOE *leaves.*

ANNIE: What did you think you're doing?!

PAT: Strike me pink!

ANNIE: Are you completely mad?!

PEARL: Calm down, Mum.

PAT: What's goin' on 'round here?

ANNIE: You're as bad as each other.

PAT: What's he...?

ANNIE: Who do you think you are? Waltzing in here stirring things up.

You got no idea, have you? No idea!

PAT: He's got no right… hang on…

ANNIE: They'll take her! Do you understand? One word from that mongrel and Welfare'll be here like a shot.

PEARL: Mum!

ANNIE: Oh, shut up, the pair of you!

*Silence.* PAT *grabs the whip.*

PAT: Come on, girl, let's show you how to use that whip properly.

*They exit. The whip cracking sounds like rifle shots.* ANNIE *slumps to the ground. She clutches at her stomach and grabs for the bucket. Outside the laugher and cracking whip form a stark contrast to* ANNIE*'s retching.*

◆ ◆ ◆ ◆ ◆

## SCENE TWELVE

*1966. A few weeks later. The river.*

*It is dusk. A beautiful sunset.* NELL *reads from a Psalm book. She has been swimming. Her clothes are bundled up nearby.*

NELL: 'Blessed is the man who walks not in the counsel of the ungodly, nor stands in the path of sinners, nor sits in the seat of the scornful;
'But his delight is in the law of the Lord, and in His law he meditates day and night.'

*A sound. It's a fish jumping. She looks up before returning to her reading.*

'He shall be like a tree…'

PAT *emerges from the river unseen by* NELL. *He wears old shorts, a face mask, and carries a handmade spear. He has a big fish on the spear. He watches her.*

'… planted by the rivers of water, that brings forth its fruit in its season, whose leaf also shall not wither, and whatever he does shall prosper.
'The ungodly are not so, but are like the chaff which the wind drives away.'

PAT: Chaff, eh?

NELL: Oh!

PAT: Relax, girl, I don't bite.

NELL: You gave me a—

PAT: She's right.

NELL: Yes, yes.

PAT: Good night for fishin', eh?

NELL: Mmm…

PAT: Full moon.

NELL: It's beautiful.

PAT: Easier to see the buggers. [*He waves the fish at her.*] Good'un, eh?

NELL: Oh, yes.

PAT: [*removing his mask*] What'd ya reckon?

NELL: Flattie?

PAT: Yeah. Plenty of tucker in this fella.

NELL: I've never been able to catch any big enough.

PAT: Probably don't know where to look.

NELL: No. I tried over there.

PAT: What ya use?

NELL: Worms.

PAT: Oh. Oughta have a go at abalone gut. Works well.

NELL: Really?

PAT: Prefer the spear meself, no waste. Only catch what you can eat.

NELL: Don't think I'd be able to spear…

PAT: Just practice. I'll show you sometime.

NELL: Would you?

PAT: 'Course. Mind if I…?

NELL: No. Please. Sit down.

PAT: Thanks. Not many of your mob get down here.

NELL: It's so peaceful.

PAT: Yeah.

NELL: I love swimming here.

PAT: This' a special place, this one here.

NELL: It is.

PAT: This is our place. My mob's place.

NELL: You own it?

PAT *laughs.*

PAT: It's our Dreaming place.

NELL: Your what?

PAT: We come from here. In the water. Our totem... Ahh, you wouldn't understand.

NELL: Go on.

PAT: You whitefellas believe all that stuff about God, eh? It's different for us. This is where we come from.

NELL: I see.

PAT: You're shivering.

NELL: It's all right.

PAT: Here, I'll warm you up.

*He puts his arm around her. She pulls away.*

Told ya, I won't bite.

NELL: My clothes...

PAT: You're a good-looking sort, you know.

NELL: Please.

PAT: Hey! I won't hurt you. Just... you know... beautiful night and everything.

NELL *rushes to her clothes.*

NELL: I better get dressed.

PAT: She's right. Promise I won't look. I'll clean this one and we can cook him up.

NELL *dresses into her habit.* PAT *cleans the fish.*

It's a good fishing hole this one. Especially when it's been dry. There's a sandbank runs halfway cross the river there. See? Can't see it when the river's full. When it's been raining the river swells up and the current gets too strong and the fishing's no good. Fish can swim over the sandbank there. Not as easy to catch 'em. At the moment it's perfect. The fish swim along the river banks like this... [*He demonstrates with his hand.*] They're either heading up the river or downstream to drop their eggs. Easier to swim against the current when there's been no rain and the current's not too strong. Then they get in here close to the river bank to look for tucker. They dive deep down into the waterholes. They can hide there under rocks and things. You won't find them if you don't know where to look. But I know where to look, eh? You like fish?

NELL: Oh, yes.

PAT: He'll cook up real good.

NELL: I'm not all that hungry.

PAT: Plenty here.

NELL: Oh…

PAT: My dad used to bring me here when I was a lad. I remember watchin' him fishin' down here. Remember that clear as a bell. We used to live in the water. Mum reckoned we'd grow gills.

NELL: When?

PAT: Long time ago. I can still see it though. Waterholes full of yabbies. Beautiful big ones. When we got sick of them we'd go down there to the beach and grab a feed of crabs or lobsters. There was this spot we knew about you could always catch lobsters. Unless the swell was running. Then we'd get mussels.

NELL: I didn't know there was so much life…

PAT: Need to educate you, eh? You dressed yet?

NELL: Yes.

*He turns to see her dressed as a nun.*

PAT: Jesus Christ!

NELL: Not quite!

PAT: Oh, my God. I… I'm sorry… I thought… I didn't know…

NELL: Don't worry. I was flattered actually.

PAT: You can't be a nun!

NELL: I am.

PAT: You don't bloody look it.

NELL: I'll help you make a fire.

PAT: Will you?

NELL: To tell you the truth, I've never eaten fresh fish before. I'd like to try some.

PAT: Hooley dooley…

NELL: You look like you've seen a ghost.

PAT: Hang about.

NELL: What?

PAT: You work down there at that convent.

NELL: Yes.

PAT: You must know me niece then.

NELL: Who's that?

PAT: Pearl Dodd.

NELL: Pearl is one of my students.

PAT: Yeah?

NELL: She brought me here. I would never have known about this if she hadn't shown me. It's my favourite place. I come here to… to think…

PAT: How's she going?

NELL: You must be Uncle Pat.

PAT: Yep.

NELL: She's very proud of you.

PAT: Pull the other one.

NELL: I can see why.

PAT: Thanks.

NELL: I mean… catching fish and… [*She picks up his spear.*] Did you make this?

PAT: Yep.

NELL: It's lovely.

PAT: It's a beauty. Never misses.

NELL: You home for long?

PAT: Never let the grass grow. Tell me. How's she gettin' on, at school?

NELL: She's very clever but…

PAT: But?

NELL: It's nothing…

PAT: What?

NELL: I worry about her.

PAT: Why?

NELL: Probably nothing but my… you know…

PAT: Nuh.

NELL: It's probably my upbringing.

PAT: Jeez, you beat around the bush, don't you?

NELL: It's just… I visited her mum.

PAT: Annie?

NELL: Yes. I'd never been on the Mission before. It was a bit of a shock.

PAT: I see.

NELL: It's not what I'm used to, but look, please, it's me, it's my…

PAT: Bit rough for you, eh?

NELL: It was so embarrassing. I thought the Mission Manager was her husband.

PAT: Yeah?

NELL: I was so embarrassed.

PAT: Why'd you think that?

NELL: Oh… silly misunderstanding. Pearl's told me so many different stories about her father…

PAT: Pulling your leg?

NELL: I always seem to put my foot in it.

PAT: She's right.

> PAT *dries himself on his shirt.*

NELL: Here. Please. Use my towel.

PAT: You sure?

NELL: Of course! It's a bit damp.

PAT: Thanks. You wanna grab some wood?

NELL: Mmm?

PAT: This' ol' fish be no good raw!

NELL: Oh, of course.

PAT: Better off startin' a fire while there's some light.

NELL: Yes. [*She gathers wood as he cleans the fish.*] Couldn't you just set lines?

PAT: You could but… but that's not the way I was taught. Fish got no chance that way, has he?

NELL: Will this be enough wood?

PAT: Nah. They're all right to start, but you need solid bits now. To make coals. No good cookin' over flame.

NELL: Oh. Sorry.

PAT: That's okay. You'll get the idea.

NELL: Oh, it's lovely here, isn't it?

PAT: Sssh. Hear that?

NELL: What?

PAT: Listen…

NELL: Sounds like someone throwing stones.

PAT: Mmm.

NELL: What is it…?

PAT: Sshh. The fish are jumping. Plenty tucker around tonight. Hey!

You're still shiverin'.

NELL: Am I? Oh yes, I'm not cold though…

PAT: Let's get that fire goin' and you can tell me all about what's been goin' on 'round here, eh?

NELL: I'm only new, remember.

PAT: You're a teacher, aren't you?

NELL: Yes but—

PAT: You're supposed to know everything then. Aren't you?

NELL: 'Supposed'.

    *Pause.*

PAT: Glad you come down here.

NELL: Me too.

PAT: Gonna tell me your name?

NELL: Oh, sorry. How rude. Helen. Nell… Nell Roberts.

PAT: Nell. My lucky day, eh?

NELL: Really?

PAT: Really.

◆ ◆ ◆ ◆ ◆

## SCENE THIRTEEN

*1966. The Mission.*

*Night. The door flies open.* JOE *staggers in. He is very drunk.*

JOE: Hey! Anyone home? Yoo-hoo… hello… [*He pulls off his boots.*] Bloody muddy out there. Me feet are freezin'. Reckon a new pair o' boots wouldn't go astray, eh? Can afford some now, thanks to that brother of yours. I was gonna have a word to the coppers but… I thought… you know… we could… do a deal. Ohh… it's cold out here. You looks nice and warm.

    *He sits on the bed. He pokes at the body lying covered in a blanket.*

Room for an old mate in there, is there? [*He stumbles to his feet and undoes his trousers.*] Jesus! Freeze the balls off a brass monkey! [*He creeps up to the bed.*] Wakey, wakey. You ready for me? Ol'

mate's come for a bit o' comfortin'. Bit of a cuddle, kiss 'n' cuddle.
Warm us up on a cold night. Lover girl! [*He falls over.*] Ohh, shit!
[*He looks over to* PEARL*'s bed.*] Come on! Piss her off... unless...
yeah... [*He pokes at the bed.*] What about something different
tonight, girls?

> *He takes a quick slug of his hip flask and leans over the bed. He*
> *is about to plant a kiss on* ANNIE *when the bedclothes are thrown*
> *back to reveal* PAT.

Jesus Christ Almighty! What the—?!

> PAT *flattens him.*

PAT: You low bastard. Get up and fight like a man.
JOE: You! I thought you'd gone...
PAT: Did you just?
JOE: Look—
PAT: Get up!
JOE: It's not like it seems.
PAT: No?
JOE: No. Really.
PAT: Go on.
JOE: You know...
PAT: No...
JOE: It's like...
PAT: What?
JOE: Christ, you're her brother...
PAT: And?
JOE: She...
PAT: Yes?
JOE: Well, she likes me... I know she's your sister and everything... but
    ... it's true.
PAT: What's true?
JOE: She gets lonely and, you know, I give her a bit of...
PAT: A bit of what?
JOE: Comfort.
PAT: That what you call it?
JOE: You're always away...
PAT: I see...

PAT *hauls him to his feet and flattens him again.*

JOE: Jesus!

PAT: On your feet.

JOE: No, please…

PAT: Fight like a man.

JOE: Don't…

PAT: Come on…

> JOE *lunges for the whip.* PAT *stamps on his hand.*

You want to be quicker than that.

> *He grabs the whip and lifts* JOE *by the handle, almost choking him.*

I paid you good money to look after her.

JOE: You're chokin' me.

PAT: Didn't I?

JOE: Let go…

PAT: You call that lookin' after her?

JOE: I can't breathe.

PAT: What have you been doing to her?

JOE: God, my throat…!

PAT: I asked you a question.

JOE: Let me go.

PAT: Answer.

JOE: I can do a deal.

PAT: Yeah?

JOE: Let me go and I promise I won't come near her again. I'll keep Welfare away for good. I won't tell anyone.

PAT: You think I believe you?

JOE: God's honour.

PAT: Whose?

JOE: Jesus! I gave you my word, didn't I?

PAT: Your word? Your word isn't worth two bob, you gutless wonder!

JOE: Please?

PAT: What were you doing in here, eh?

JOE: Nothin'.

PAT: Nothing? [*He tightens his grip.*] What?

JOE: You know…
PAT: Say it!
JOE: Hey! Don't! Please…
PAT: You like it, tough guy?
JOE: I swear. Jesus, I helped her keep her girl…
PAT: You helped her?
JOE: I did… hey!
PAT: What?
JOE: They woulda taken her away if it wasn't for me.
PAT: Yeah?
JOE: Yeah, I been good to her…
PAT: You raped her.
JOE: No!
PAT: Go on, admit it!
JOE: Please… I beg you… she… she wanted it…
PAT: She what?
JOE: She did…
PAT: You…

> *He lifts* JOE *with the whip handle, strangling him as he lifts.*

JOE: Aaarrgh…
PAT: You fuckin' piece of shit!
JOE: [*choking*] You… kill me… they'll… aargh… they'll know…
   they'll know… it's you…
PAT: [*tightening his grip*] Shut up!

> *As* PAT *squeezes the last drop of life out of* JOE, PEARL *rushes in.*

PEARL: Uncle Pat!

> PAT *freezes.*

Mum's sick. She collapsed.

> *Finally* PAT *drops* JOE *who writhes on the floor in agony.*

PAT: What?!

> *He rushes to her.*

PEARL: We were waiting for you, like you said… [*She sees* JOE *writhing
   on the floor.*] What have you…?
PAT: Don't worry about him… he won't bother you again…

JOE *seizes the opportunity to crawl out.*

PEARL: She's real crook, Uncle Pat.

PAT: Where—?

PEARL: Sister Helen took her to the hospital.

PAT: To the hospital?

PEARL: I'm scared.

PAT: She'll be right there. Now, listen here, girl…

PEARL: What?

PAT: I can't stop here now.

PEARL: But what are we going to do…?

PAT: Hell… I gotta go, girl… that bugger'll be onto the cops… they'll put me away. I can't go back… not again. You get up to that hospital and look after your mother.

PEARL: Don't go…

PAT: You hear?

PEARL: Uncle Pat…

PAT: Got to, bub. Got to. Look after her!

*He rushes off.*

PEARL: No!

◆ ◆ ◆ ◆ ◆

*SCENE FOURTEEN*

*1966. Two weeks later. The country railway station.*

PEARL *waits for a train. Beside her is a suitcase.* NELL *stands beside her.*

NELL: You've got your ticket?

PEARL: Yes.

NELL: Now remember. You'll be picked up at Central Station by one of the nuns. The guard will make sure you change trains at Byron Bay for Sydney. It's the North Coast Mail. Remember? The North Coast Mail.

PEARL: Can't you come with me?

NELL: I'm sorry.

PEARL: I'm scared.

NELL: Of course you're scared.

PEARL: I wish we could find Uncle Pat.

NELL: I know.

PEARL: He's always disappearing when we need him.

NELL: I think he had to… under the circumstances… you know… make himself scarce.

PEARL: I don't want to go away.

NELL: You can't stay here by yourself. Trust me, Pearl. This is for the best.

PEARL: When will I see you?

NELL: In a few weeks.

PEARL: You promise?

NELL: I promise.

*The sound of the approaching train.*

I will pray for you every night.

PEARL: Mum!

*The train whistle. Blackout.*

## END OF ACT ONE

# ACT TWO

## SCENE ONE

*A funeral.*

*A shaft of sunlight isolates a man (*BRIAN*) in mourning clothes. He delivers a eulogy[2] at a graveside service.*

BRIAN: 'And thou art dead, as young and fair
　　As aught of mortal birth;
　　And form so soft, and charms so rare,
　　Too soon returned to Earth!
　　Though Earth received them in her bed,
　　And o'er the spot the crowd may tread
　　In carelessness or mirth,
　　There is an eye which could not brook
　　A moment on that grave to look.'

　　*A seagull's squawk breaks the moment. He continues.*

Lord Byron's words express the way I feel at the moment. My own would not do the occasion justice. Thank you, Pearl, for the beautiful thought. If you would give us a moment alone we will see you back at the house where we can celebrate the life of this wonderful human being.

　　BRIAN *is joined by* PEARL, *now 20. They hug. It is 1975.*

PEARL: Oh, Dad!
BRIAN: Pearl.
PEARL: I can't handle this.
BRIAN: It's all right.
PEARL: Hold me. [*Pause.*] Thank you.
BRIAN: Thank *you*.
PEARL: I don't know how to… do this…
BRIAN: You're doing fine.

---

[2] Lord Byron, *And Thou Art Dead, As Young and Fair*.

PEARL: I wasn't prepared for how I'd feel.

BRIAN: At times like this none of us can tell how we'll respond.

PEARL: It's so confusing.

BRIAN: I know.

PEARL: No you don't!

BRIAN: Pardon?

PEARL: I keep thinking of my mother. My birth mother.

BRIAN: I see.

PEARL: It's not out of disrespect to Jennifer.

BRIAN: Of course not.

PEARL: This is the first funeral I've been to.

BRIAN: Oh?

PEARL: I wasn't allowed to go to my mum's…

BRIAN: I suppose they thought you were too young.

PEARL: Now I've lost two mothers.

BRIAN: Pearl…

PEARL: Two dead mothers!

BRIAN: Darling…

PEARL: It isn't fair.

BRIAN: I know.

PEARL: It's like I've done something wrong, jumped in the wrong river.

BRIAN: I'll look after you. We have to stick together.

PEARL: I can see why Uncle Pat never settled down.

BRIAN: What?

PEARL: Ever seen a horse getting broken?

BRIAN: No.

PEARL: Takes forever.

BRIAN: Yes, yes.

PEARL: You've broken me in.

BRIAN: I wouldn't put it quite like that…

PEARL: 'Some horses are so badly broken in, that all the thrashings break their spirit and they just give up.'

BRIAN: You've got to put all that behind you.

PEARL: Be easy, wouldn't it?

BRIAN: What would?

PEARL: To run with the mob.

BRIAN: We've got to get you through those exams, that's what we've got to do.

PEARL: How can you be so strong?

BRIAN: I try and keep my eye on the ball, that's all.

PEARL: You're a Stoic!

BRIAN: You can't worry about the dropped catches and the bad shots and the poor decisions. You've just got to steel yourself for the next delivery.

PEARL: I hate cricket!

BRIAN: We should be going.

PEARL: Look!

BRIAN: Seagulls.

PEARL: Flying off with Jennifer's spirit?

BRIAN: She would have loved that idea.

PEARL: I loved her, Dad, she was so good to me. You've both... since... you know... you've both been... great.

BRIAN: We were blessed that you came to us.

PEARL: The seagulls are circling. Mullet must be running.

BRIAN: The caterers will be waiting.

PEARL: Of course! The caterers.

◆ ◆ ◆ ◆ ◆

*SCENE TWO*

*1975. A boxing gym. Redfern.*

PAT *wears a Rabbitoh (South Sydney) rugby league beanie.*

PAT: All right, you boys, now listen here. Hey! You sit down and listen to me or I'll box your bloody ears. You hear me? Right-oh. Who's heard of Cassius Clay? Only a few. Muhammed Ali? All of youse. Know the difference? Clay was Ali's slave name. Ali is the name he wears as proudly as this... [*He lifts his shirt and points to his skin.*] When I was in the Boys' Home they took my name away and give me a number. Number Forty-Two. But I learnt to fight, didn't I? In the tents they called me Black Billy the Dancer 'cause I moved so quick. Like Muhammed Ali and Lionel Rose. No one could lay a glove on me and now I'm just Pat. You want to box? Okay. The stance. Get side-on. Like this. Gives 'em less of a target and you're in a better position to throw a punch. See? If you're square-on you're an easy mark and the punch can't be disguised, can it? Okay. Side-on. Hands up. Always keep your hands up. Only the great Muhammed Ali's good enough to drop his hands and none of youse could hold a candle to him no matter what you think. Tuck your chin in otherwise you're presenting an easy target. Like this, see? Up on your toes. So you can move. Never sit back on your heels or you'll end up flat on your back. You've got to be fit. None of you is fit. When I come in before I seen two of you lighting up a smoke. Fighters don't smoke. They don't drink neither. You wanna fight then clean up your act. Plenty of roadwork. Sit-ups. Push-ups. Like this. Old bloke like me can do 'em, so can you. On to the bag and the rope and when you're fit enough we'll toss you into the ring and see how good you are. Right-oh. Off you go. 'Round the park twice and back you come. No cutting corners neither. First one back gets to spar with me. Away you go!

◆ ◆ ◆ ◆ ◆

*SCENE THREE*

*1975. Central Station.*

NELL, *dressed as a civilian, waits under the clock.*

P.A.: [*voice-over*] The train from platform twenty-three, the North Coast Mail, will be departing in twenty minutes. First stop Strathfield then Hornsby, Newcastle, Coff's Harbour, Grafton, Lismore and Byron Bay. Change at Byron Bay for the Sunshine Coast, then on to Brisbane.

NELL: My God!

BRIAN *enters.*

BRIAN: Helen?
NELL: Nell.
BRIAN: Brian. How do you do? [*Pause.*] Are you all right?
NELL: Yes, yes. The North Coast Mail.
BRIAN: Pardon?
NELL: Ghosts.

BRIAN: Been waiting long?

NELL: No…

BRIAN: Sorry I'm late. Got caught up. Listening to the news. Did you hear? The Governor General's sacked the government.

NELL: Thanks for coming.

BRIAN: [*looking up*] The old clock, eh? Can't miss it. I imagine this is a bit of meeting place for country people. And others.

NELL: Yes.

BRIAN: Good to keep these things on neutral ground.

NELL: How is she?

BRIAN: Excellent.

NELL: It's nearly ten years…

BRIAN: Did very well in her exams. Passed with flying colours!

NELL: Oh?

BRIAN: Law. Third year.

NELL: Really?

BRIAN: She has a bright future.

NELL: That's wonderful.

BRIAN: I'm very proud of her.

NELL: Of course.

BRIAN: You were her teacher?

NELL: For a short time.

BRIAN: You must have taught her well.

NELL: I was very young.

BRIAN: We all have to start somewhere.

NELL: I… I've been trying for years… to find her. To track her down.

BRIAN: You said in your letter.

NELL: I was hoping she might come…

BRIAN: I see.

NELL: I have to talk to her… to explain…

BRIAN: I don't think that's a good idea.

NELL: You don't understand.

BRIAN: I do.

NELL: No, I have to talk to her. It's important for me as well.

BRIAN: Yes. I'm sure you are on some sort of a crusade, but in this case your enthusiasm is misplaced. Pearl is in no need of assistance. The road before her is uncluttered. She doesn't need any obstacles in her way.

NELL: She's got to know… I've been trying to find her mother too.

BRIAN: Her birth mother?

NELL: Annie. No trace of her anywhere.

BRIAN: She's dead.

NELL: Dead?

BRIAN: Yes.

NELL: You sure…?

BRIAN: Of course I'm sure! I've got her death certificate. When Pearl came to us they sent us a copy.

NELL: Oh no.

BRIAN: You see? That chapter is closed.

NELL: When…?

BRIAN: Look. I appreciate your interest, but at this stage of her life the last thing Pearl needs is someone dredging up the past. She's been through quite enough. She's presently coping with the death of her foster mother, she's finished her exams. She doesn't need any more trauma.

NELL: Have you met her uncle?

BRIAN: Didn't you hear me?

NELL: Pat.

BRIAN: Take your letter back. We won't be needing it. We won't be hearing from you again either. Do you understand? We're putting the past behind us. Where it belongs. I'm sure you mean well but you would be better served helping those in real need. You can't rewrite history but you can influence the future. If you are really serious about it why don't you contact someone at Freedom From Hunger? They do need your help.

NELL: You can't…

BRIAN: Here. Read this. It's from an essay she wrote on the subject of religion a few years ago. I photocopied it. Goodbye.

*He exits.*

NELL: [*reading*] 'I once befriended a nun. She gave me hope and love and shaped the way I saw the world. She introduced me to poetry and I showed her the bush. She was once my guiding light but now that light's gone out.'

◆ ◆ ◆ ◆ ◆

*SCENE FOUR*

*1977. A squash court.*

BRIAN: Out!

PEARL: What?

BRIAN: It was out.

PEARL: Out?

BRIAN: Yes. Out.

PEARL: No it wasn't.

BRIAN: It was.

PEARL: No way.

BRIAN: Oh, come on…

PEARL: What do you mean?

BRIAN: It was clearly out.

PEARL: Bullshit.

BRIAN: Pearl…

PEARL: It didn't look out to me.

BRIAN: It was below the line.

PEARL: You're kidding?

BRIAN: You can see.

PEARL: Where?

BRIAN: There.

PEARL: There? That's not it.

BRIAN: Look, it was out.

PEARL: Just because you say so.

BRIAN: Are you accusing me of cheating?

PEARL: I'm not accusing you of anything.

BRIAN: Well, you are.

PEARL: I'm just telling you that shot was above the line.

BRIAN: What's got into you?

PEARL: Nothing.

BRIAN: It's only a game.

PEARL: Exactly.

BRIAN: You are accusing me of cheating.

PEARL: Depends which way you call it, I suppose.

BRIAN: Oh, for God's sake, grow up!

PEARL: Me?

BRIAN: You've been like a bear with a sore head for weeks.

PEARL: Crap.

BRIAN: What is it?

PEARL: Nothing. Let's play the point again then.

BRIAN: No way, I won fair and square.

PEARL: You're always right, aren't you?

BRIAN: Not always. Just this time.

PEARL: Sure.

BRIAN: This is silly.

PEARL: Yeah, yeah. It's always silly when I question something.

BRIAN: What are you going on about?

PEARL: Can't trust a black person, can you?

*Pause.*

BRIAN: That's unfair.

PEARL: Is it?

BRIAN: You know it is.

PEARL: I don't know anything. That's the trouble.

BRIAN: Pearl…

PEARL: What the fuck am I meant to think? Eh?

BRIAN: I wouldn't cheat…

PEARL: I went for that interview for my Articles and they took me to lunch. All this small talk about family and stuff. I didn't know what to say. I felt stupid.

BRIAN: Why?

PEARL: Because I don't even know where I come from.

BRIAN: Pearl…

PEARL: Look at me. I'm a bloody nobody, aren't I?

BRIAN: Don't be crazy.

PEARL: I'm going crazy.

BRIAN: Hey, hey.

PEARL: It's all right for you. You're not black.

BRIAN: The colour of your skin's got nothing to do…

PEARL: It's not my skin I'm talking about, it's my heart.

BRIAN: I thought we talked about this.

PEARL: Oh yes, we talked all right, but that doesn't solve anything. I can't ignore what's happening around me just because I've got a bloody law degree.

BRIAN: Your law degree will enable you to do something constructive.

PEARL: I want to know. Do you understand? Is it so strange that I might like to know who I am? Where I come from. Look at me. What am I meant to think? All this shit! It's driving me mad. God! I don't know what's going on anymore.

BRIAN: Don't…

PEARL: I don't even know who my father is. He could be anyone. [*Pause.*] I mean… my… my real father.

BRIAN: I know.

PEARL: Oh… shit… I'm sorry…

BRIAN: It's all right.

PEARL: I didn't mean to have a go at you…

BRIAN: No.

PEARL: It's just…

BRIAN: Let's play the point again.

PEARL: Please, I didn't mean… to say that. That's not what I meant. You've done everything for me. I love you more than anything. It's hard.

BRIAN: I know.

PEARL: Forgive me?

BRIAN: Of course.

PEARL: Double or nothing?

BRIAN: Double or nothing?

PEARL: You've got to give me a chance to get back.

BRIAN: Don't you ever give up?

PEARL: No.

BRIAN: If you're as tough in Court as you are on the court, pity help the legal fraternity!

PEARL: My serve?

BRIAN: Mine I think.

PEARL: Toss you for it…

> *She tosses her lucky coin.*

BRIAN: Tails.

PEARL: Heads!

BRIAN: You win!

PEARL: 'Course!

*She prepares to serve.*

❖ ❖ ❖ ❖ ❖

*SCENE FIVE*

*1985. The Redfern gym.*

PAT *spars, shadow boxing. He wears South Sydney colours.*

PAT: Jab, jab, jab. Hook! Jab, jab jab. Right cross! Bob, weave, bob, weave…

> NELL *enters. She stops and watches him.*

Jab, jab, jab. Uppercut! Combination—left, right, left, right. Whoa! Sorry, love. Gym's closed. [*He continues his workout.*] This's a proper gym. The trendy one's down the street. You're the second one this week, you know. A young sort come in the other day. Good looker too. Wearin' this tiny little… [*He sees who it is.*] Shit! Oh! Fuck! Oh, sorry…

NELL: Pat?

PAT: Bugger me dead!

NELL: It is you!

PAT: Sister Helen?

NELL: Not Sister anymore, just Nell.

PAT: Gawd! [*Pause.*] Feels like someone's walkin' on me grave.

NELL: I was looking for the Medical Service.

PAT: Next block.

NELL: I'm hopeless at following directions!

PAT: Yeah?

NELL: Luckily!

PAT: Never thought I'd clap eyes on you again.

NELL: No, me either.

PAT: What do you reckon?

NELL: Sorry?

> *He spars.*

PAT: Pretty sharp, eh?

NELL: Very.

PAT: Here. [*He pats his stomach.*] Hit that!

NELL: What?

PAT: Go on.

NELL: Hit you?

PAT: Give us your best!

NELL: No!

PAT: Why not? Embarrassed?

NELL: Of course not!

PAT: Well? Have a go then.

>*She taps his stomach.*

That the best you can do? Go on.

>*Finally she winds up and hits him as hard as she can. He laughs.*

Hard as a rock, eh?

NELL: Yes…

PAT: Gotta stay on top of the young'uns. Training 'em up. Coupla good young fighters amongst 'em too. Keeps 'em off the streets, eh?

NELL: God, Pat…

PAT: Swearing now!

NELL: You look fantastic.

PAT: Scrubbed up all right yourself. Where you been?

NELL: Been? Oh. India, actually.

PAT: Savin' the poor?

NELL: You know…

PAT: Big job there.

NELL: Yes.

PAT: Shoudda looked me up earlier.

NELL: I didn't know where to look. [*Pause.*] The truth is I gave up years ago.

PAT: Eh?

NELL: Trying to find you.

PAT: Never toss the towel in!

NELL: No.

PAT: Never know what's…

NELL: You don't! [*Pause.*] Do you ever go back up there, to the coast?

PAT: Nah. They built a big tourist resort there. No more fish.

NELL: Of course.

PAT: City fella now.

NELL: What about Pearl?

PAT: The one that got away.

NELL: How is she?

PAT: On a good paddock that one.

NELL: Have you seen her?

PAT: I know where she is.

NELL: Of course you do.

PAT: Gotta let some brumbies find their own way back to the mob. Can't force 'em. Some make it. Some don't. That's the way of it.

NELL: I wish I could see her.

PAT: To confess?

NELL: Yes. Confess.

PAT: Then the wounds'll heal, eh?

NELL: Maybe.

PAT: You whitefellas!

NELL: Hopeless.

PAT: Say that again.

NELL: I've got a lot of ground to make up.

PAT: Yep.

NELL: Will you help me?

PAT: Up to her.

NELL: I'm so sorry, Pat. When her stepdad told me about Annie…

PAT: Eh?

NELL: About her death.

PAT: Yeah?

NELL: I was frightened that you…

PAT: Me! Take a good'un to put me down!

NELL: Can you tell me where Annie's buried? I'd like to pay my respects.

PAT: Jeez, girl, you don't know nothin', do you?

NELL: I thought I did. Once. Do you… ever think… about those times…?

PAT: Not really. Water's a bit muddy.

NELL: Please help me, Pat.

PAT: I'll do what I can.

NELL: Thank you.

PAT: Never know your luck in a big city, eh?

◆ ◆ ◆ ◆ ◆

*SCENE SIX*

*1985. The bush.*

*An Aboriginal woman sweeps leaves from in front of her caravan. She looks older than her years. It's* ANNIE. *She brushes her doll's hair.*

ANNIE: That's a girl. You go to sleep now. No more cryin', bub. Mummy's here. Mummy'll look after you. They all think I don't know what's goin' on. That's what they think. Ha! Let 'em think what they like. Then they'll leave me be, won't they, bub? They won't come near us, will they? No one bothers about a stray, do they? They're only interested in the thoroughbreds and I'm no bloody thoroughbred, that's for sure! [*She taps her head.*] But, I've still got this, see, and no one knows what goes on inside here! You need this. Gets you through all sorts of... stuff. [*She gestures.*] That's why you gotta do your homework, bub. So you can use this. Get so far in front o' the mob the rest can't see you for dust. Yeah! They'll clap the winners and shoot the losers. Like your bloody, useless Uncle Pat says, 'Never give a sucker an even break'. You hear? Watch your back, girl, stay out there in front of the pack and don't look over your shoulder. Head down, arse up, flat chat, full steam ahead. No one's gonna keep up with you!

◆ ◆ ◆ ◆ ◆

*SCENE SEVEN*

*1985.*

PEARL *argues her case in court.*

PEARL: Well, the point is, Your Honour, my client has every right to see his children. At present he is being hindered in doing so by the other party. All we are seeking are Orders that allow for reasonable Access. No one would deny that it is important for all children to have regular contact with their parents. We are seeking Orders that provide for Access for my client every second weekend from 6 p.m. Friday to 6 p.m. Sunday. Secondly, we seek Access on alternate holidays so my client can have a period of uninterrupted time with his children. Thirdly, two hours on Father's Day. Fourthly, reasonable access on their birthdays, say three hours, and finally, alternate Christmases.

We would stress, Your Honour, that it is the children who are suffering from the other party's recalcitrance in this matter. It is their welfare we aim to protect. This is a simple Access matter which has nothing to do with Custody. We wish to assure the other party that there will be no challenge to the Custody arrangements now in place. We would like this matter settled as expeditiously as possible to prevent any further damage occurring to the children's relationship with their father.

Thank you, Your Honour.

◆ ◆ ◆ ◆ ◆

*SCENE EIGHT*

*1985. The bush.*

ANNIE *sits swatting flies with a slow, mechanical action. The sound of dogs offstage. She pays scant attention to them as she nurses her baby doll. Suddenly she grabs an old broom.*

ANNIE: Get out of it, you bloody mongrel. Go on! Get out of it. I'll give it to you!

*She sits. After a few moments* PAT *rushes on carrying a box of stores.*

PAT: Sis!

*She stares at him.*

Hey, sis.

*She turns away.*

Come on, sis…

ANNIE: Go away.

PAT: Couldn't find you.

ANNIE: You deaf or something?

PAT: Don't be like that.

*She ignores him.*

I was lookin' for you up there. Wish you'd stay in one spot. Old Joey Duncan told me you'd moved camp. [*He looks around.*] Good here though. Close to the creek. Any fish? You oughta drop a line…

ANNIE *busies herself, deliberately ignoring him.*

'Spose you don't want me news?

*No reply.*

Oh well, suit yourself.

*A standoff. Finally she relents.*

ANNIE: What news?

PAT: I seen her.

ANNIE: What do you mean? I told you to keep away from her. Leave her be.

PAT: Settle down—

ANNIE: You go near her I'll never talk to you again. You hear? She don't need you messin' her up anymore. You had your chance. You leave her alone. She's got a new life now. She don't need you buggerin' it up.

PAT: But—

ANNIE: You done enough trouble making. You leave Pearl out of it. She's going places, she don't need you interfering.

PAT: Sis…

ANNIE: Don't you 'sis' me! That girl's got a chance to live a decent life, she don't need us gettin' in the way.

PAT: I'm not talkin' about Pearl.

ANNIE: Eh?

PAT: Never bloody listen do you?

ANNIE: No bloody good listenin' to you!

PAT: I seen Nell. Sister Helen. From the old days.

ANNIE: What's she want?

PAT: To see you…

ANNIE: I'm not seein' no one.

PAT: She needs—

*She hits him with the broom.*

Oi!

ANNIE: Piss off!

PAT: Don't!

ANNIE: Get!

PAT: Hey!

*She chases him.*

Annie!

ANNIE: Shooo!

*He grabs the broom.*

PAT: Stop it!

ANNIE: Leave me alone.

PAT: It's time…

ANNIE: That's all I want you to do. Just leave me alone.

PAT: Please, sis…

ANNIE: Can't you even do that for me? Can't you?

PAT: I'll tell her you're not ready yet.

ANNIE: Tell her what you like.

PAT: Here.

*He gives her the box of stores.*

Keep you goin' for a while.

ANNIE: Rack off.

*She forces him off.*

PAT: See you in a month or so.

ANNIE: Yeah, yeah.

PAT: Promise.

*He goes.*

ANNIE: Your promise isn't worth two bob. [*She sits the doll and begins sweeping.*] You just lie there, I'll get you a feed in a sec. Okay? That's a girl. Gotta keep the place tidy, eh bub? That's the main thing. Sweep up the mess… sweep up the mess. [*She stops suddenly.*] Pearl!

❖ ❖ ❖ ❖ ❖

*SCENE NINE*

*1988. Lady Macquarie's Chair overlooking Sydney Harbour.*

PEARL *and* BRIAN *share a picnic.*

BRIAN: What a beautiful day!

PEARL: Shame I have to go back to work.

BRIAN: 'No rest for the wicked.'

PEARL: Get out of it!

BRIAN: Gee, the Tall Ships are going to look pretty impressive coming through the Heads, aren't they?

PEARL: Depends whose side you're on I suppose.

BRIAN: Champagne?

> *He pours her a glass.*

PEARL: Why not? Don't get a promotion every day! Actually, one of the partners reckons, this is top secret, he reckons if I keep going the way I am, that they'll offer me a junior partnership.

BRIAN: Good.

PEARL: Dad?

BRIAN: Mmm?

PEARL: What's the matter?

BRIAN: Nothing. Do you… do you ever think about your mother?

PEARL: My birth mother?

BRIAN: Yes.

PEARL: It's weird you know. I had this dream about her. She was sitting alone in one of those old dog boxes that used to be on country trains. Holding a suitcase on her lap. Smiling. It was like the train I came to Sydney on. Why do you ask?

BRIAN: Do you remember Sister Helen?

PEARL: Yes, why?

BRIAN: I'm not happy about this…

PEARL: What?

BRIAN: She wants to see you.

PEARL: I don't want to see her.

BRIAN: No. I didn't think you would. The fact is I can't stop her. Not anymore. She found out where you worked. I tried to persuade her but…

NELL *enters.*

... here she is.

PEARL: Sister Helen?

NELL: Hello, Pearl.

PEARL: What are you...?

NELL: I had to see you.

PEARL: Don't come near me.

NELL: Pearl...

PEARL: What do you want?

BRIAN: Tell her.

PEARL: What? Tell me what?

BRIAN: What are you waiting for?

NELL: Your mother is still alive.

PEARL: What?

NELL: Annie.

PEARL: Eh?

NELL: Annie is still alive, Pearl.

PEARL: Dad?

BRIAN: It's true.

PEARL: My birth mother is alive?

NELL: Yes.

PEARL: You're joking.

NELL: No. I'm not.

PEARL: She can't be...

BRIAN: It appears she is.

PEARL: But... when I... she died in hospital... after that night Uncle
    Pat bashed... It can't be true... Jesus Christ! What's going on here?

NELL: I'm sorry.

PEARL: You're sorry?

NELL: I... I know what I did was wrong.

PEARL: What is this?

BRIAN: Get on with it.

NELL: I... we... lied to you. We didn't tell you the truth.

PEARL: Well?

NELL: Your mother... Annie... had an ectopic pregnancy.

PEARL: I know that! It killed her... I thought... you told...

NELL: That's what we told you.

PEARL: What?

NELL: To protect you.

PEARL: Protect me?

NELL: After she collapsed she was in a coma, for days. She did nearly die. It was... there was... chaos. The police were after Pat, he disappeared. Joe reported the whole thing to the Welfare. They were coming to get you. You could have been sent anywhere.

PEARL: You're incredible.

NELL: We, the school, we arranged for you to go to Saint Margaret's. I knew they'd take care of you. It was all I could think of. The Welfare agreed as long as no one contacted you. We decided... we thought... the best thing was to tell you she'd died.

PEARL: Did you know about this?

BRIAN: No. We were told you were an orphan... I always believed... Oh, Pearl...

NELL: I traced the death certificate, it was a forgery. Brian couldn't have known. Death certificates were forged all the time to stop families re-uniting.

PEARL: And...

NELL: When Annie finally recovered I... I lied to her. I told her no one knew where you were, that Welfare had taken you away. I convinced her not to try and find you. I told her that you would be moved to somewhere terrible if she contacted you. To protect you she must let you go. If she loved you she must never see you again.

PEARL: She believed you?

NELL: She had no choice. It broke her heart but... I've never forgiven myself.

PEARL: When did you find out about this?

BRIAN: A few years ago.

PEARL: A few years ago?!

BRIAN: Yes. I couldn't bring myself to tell you. I thought it best to... to move on.

NELL: Pat—

PEARL: Uncle Pat? You've seen Uncle Pat?

NELL: Yes...

PEARL: When?

NELL: A couple of times.

PEARL: Does he…? Hang on…

NELL: He knows where she is. He won't tell me.

PEARL: You know how to find him?

NELL: Yes.

PEARL: Why didn't he contact me?

NELL: I don't—

PEARL: What the fuck is going on here?

> BRIAN *attacks* NELL.

BRIAN: You see?

NELL: She has to know the truth.

BRIAN: Who are you to judge? I warned you! I told you what this would do to us. I told you!

NELL: Pearl, trust me—

PEARL: Trust you? Trust you! You'd be the last person on earth I would trust. I will never forget that train trip. I cried all the way to the city. I cried for days. It was a nightmare. There was a woman in a blue hat sitting opposite me, she had a suitcase on her lap. She just stared at me. I'm sure she thought I was running away. I kept thinking Welfare would grab me and take me. At every stop I froze expecting any minute to be dragged back to the Girls' Home. Then the nuns collected me from Central. You can imagine how that made me feel! I hated that boarding school.

I kept expecting you to turn up. You promised, remember? You promised you'd come. On weekends when the other boarders went on leave I kept praying you'd show up, but you didn't, did you? I used to pretend someone was coming for me and I'd hide in the bushes until the Matron finally caught me. I hated everything until my foster parents came along and rescued me. It if it wasn't for them I wouldn't be standing here now.

You were responsible for what I went through. You promised you'd write and come and see me and… what? Nothing. Not a word. So, here you are twenty-two years later. Two hundred years after the White Invasion. Coming to me for absolution!

NELL: Dear Pearl…

PEARL: Appeasing your guilt?

NELL: I suppose.

PEARL: Are you for real?

NELL: I'm sorry.

PEARL: What do you want me to do? Forgive you? Make you feel better?

NELL: No, no. I wanted to explain.

PEARL: You've waited all this time?

NELL: I didn't know what to do.

BRIAN: I tried to stop her from her seeing you. To protect you.

NELL: Pearl, I had to tell you. In person.

PEARL: You come near me again and I'll get a Restraining Order. Understand?

NELL: Don't…

PEARL: How dare you!

BRIAN: You've said enough.

NELL: Pearl…

> NELL *approaches her.*

PEARL: Don't you come near me. Get away. Don't you dare touch me!

NELL: I made a terrible mistake, Pearl. I know you won't believe this, but I thought I was helping you… I've destroyed everything. I know. But Pat and your mother, they were innocent, Pearl. Their hands were tied.

PEARL: You fucken bitch!

> PEARL *attacks* NELL. *It is an attack that resonates with* PAT*'s attack on* JOE.

BRIAN: Pearl!

> BRIAN *tries to grab her. She lashes out at him. Finally he restrains her. He turns on* NELL.

I hope you're pleased with yourself.

NELL: Oh, Pearl…

PEARL: Fuck off!

NELL: I'm so sorry.

> NELL *runs off.* PEARL *collapses.*

PEARL: Oh!

BRIAN: Darling girl…

PEARL: What am I going to do?

BRIAN: We'll sort it out.

PEARL: Why didn't they contact me?

BRIAN: If we talk it through…

PEARL: Why did they let me believe this… this bullshit?

BRIAN: Darling…

PEARL: Darling? How can you…? You… you're just as bad. I put my faith in you. You were the one person I knew I could rely on. You were the one person who would tell me the truth, who would never betray me.

BRIAN: But—

PEARL: My God. You've known for… for three years?

BRIAN: Yes but…

PEARL: How could you?

BRIAN: Because…

PEARL: Because what?

BRIAN: Because I didn't want to lose you.

PEARL: Please go.

BRIAN: Darling…

PEARL: Please?

BRIAN: Let me explain.

PEARL: No. Your words are meaningless. Understand? Meaningless.

*After a moment* BRIAN *exits.*

What do I do now? What is going on? Ohh… Mum!

◆ ◆ ◆ ◆ ◆

*SCENE TEN*

*1988. The bush.*

ANNIE: Go on, get! Off you go. Get out of here. Bloody things. No bloody good to no one. Are they, bub? Hey! I'm watching you. Yes I am. Skinny-lookin' thing. Don't think I don't know what you're up to. Shoo. [*She freezes.*] Who's there? Careful. I got me broom. Don't try… Ah, bugger it. [*She is about to sit.*] Eh, you girl! Careful of that sandbank. Keep away from there. Don't trust it. It'll give way on you and then… whoosh!… down you go, way down. Big current there. Big undertow. Watch it or you'll be washed away.

It's deeper than you think. It's no good, that one, you can't see the bottom. What you lookin' at, dog? You lookin' at me, eh? What you see, dog? Not much I reckon. Don't worry. I got me eye on you too. You and me. Same boat, eh? Only I'm smarter than you, you mangy-lookin' thing. Way smarter. Don't forget it, all right? I know all about dogs like you. Seen plenty. [*She laughs.*] Plenty of tricks left in this old dog, don't you worry about that.

*She throws something at the dog.*

That's it! Off you go. Tail between your legs. Ahh, bugger it. No bloody good to nobody. No bloody good to nobody.

*She lies on the ground, covering herself with an old blanket , cuddling her doll. The sound off of a bus. Laughter. Horns blowing. Catcalls.* PAT *rushes on.*

PAT: Sis?

ANNIE: What's the bloody racket?

PAT: G'day, sis.

ANNIE: What do you want?

PAT: Got a bus here, sis.

ANNIE: Bus?

PAT: Yeah. Takin' everyone down the city for the big march.

ANNIE: What are you talking about?

PAT: Invasion Day, sis. All us blackfellas gonna march—

ANNIE: Piss off.

PAT: People are comin' from all over the place. It's gonna be…

ANNIE: Shoo!

PAT: … the biggest corroboree ever. Them whitefellas won't know what hit 'em! When them Tall Ships come through the Heads…

*The horn sounds.*

… we'll send 'em back this time.

ANNIE: You have yourself on, don't you?

PAT: Coming?

ANNIE: Bugger off!

PAT: Do you good.

ANNIE: I'm not goin' nowhere.

VOICE: [*offstage*] Come on, Annie! Come on, Pat, get a move on. We'll miss the bloody march!

PAT: Please come, sis.

ANNIE: Off you go.

PAT: C'mon, sis.

ANNIE: Leave me be, will you?

PAT: You coming or not?

ANNIE: No.

PAT: Everyone else is. You can't stop here by yourself.

ANNIE: Never worried you before.

PAT: You could see Pearl.

ANNIE: She don't want to see me. Like this. Leave her alone. You hear?

*The horn. Shouts.*

Let sleeping dogs lie.

*She lies down.*

PAT: Have it your own way then. You're missin' out... Don't blame me... stubborn, bloody thing...

*He exits. The bus takes off. Loud celebratory noises.* ANNIE *starts to cough.*

ANNIE: Blood. [*She coughs.*] Gawd, bub. Fallin' apart I am. [*She picks up the doll.*] You'll look after me, won't you? Better than them bloody doctors they tried to get me to see. Don't trust them. Never know what they'll tell you. [*She coughs again, before suddenly shouting after the bus.*] Piss off and leave me be. Nothin' but bloody trouble, you are! No good to me. Comin' and goin' like the bloody wind. All you've ever done. You're as bad as those bloody dogs.

*She picks up a stone and throws it at a dog.*

You piss off too, you mangy-lookin' thing. I don't need nobody. Nobody.

*She starts coughing uncontrollably.*

◆ ◆ ◆ ◆ ◆

*SCENE ELEVEN*

*1990. Redfern. Night.*

PEARL *stands outside a house in Eveleigh Street. She knocks. A* MAN *watches from the shadows.*

PEARL: Come on. [*She knocks again.*] Hello? [*She looks around nervously before trying again.*] Anyone home?

> The MAN *steps out of the shadows.* PEARL *knocks once more. No reply. She turns and sees the* MAN.

Oh!

> The MAN *approaches. It's* PAT.

Please… I… haven't got… [*She fishes in her wallet.*] Here…

> *She offers money.*

It's all I've—
PAT: Can I help you?
PEARL: Help? Oh. No. Um…
PAT: You look a bit toey…
PEARL: Yes… I'm… it's all right.
PAT: Who you lookin' for?
PEARL: Don't worry, I'll come back tomorrow.
PAT: Calm down. I'm not gonna hurt you.
PEARL: Oh no… I didn't think…
PAT: Yes you did. You thought I was gonna mug you, eh?
PEARL: No, no. I just got a bit of a fright…
PAT: You after ol' Mrs Gorrie?
PEARL: Ah… yes… actually, that's right.
PAT: She's not in.
PEARL: It doesn't appear so.
PAT: Won't get much change out of her at the moment. She's down the pub. Full as the last bus.
PEARL: Hell!
PAT: What's the story?
PEARL: Her son's in trouble. He's down at the police station.
PAT: Snatchin' bags?
PEARL: Yes. If I can get his mother to come we can arrange bail… otherwise… I'm sorry. This isn't your problem…
PAT: My word it is. It's everyone's problem.
PEARL: I work for Legal Aid…

PAT: I know!

PEARL: What?

PAT: This mob o' fish. Swimmin' along like this, see? Swimmin' along near the bank, lookin' for tucker. This little one got caught in a net. The rest of the mob kept swimmin', some gettin' caught and others gettin' away. They kept goin' upstream till the big rain came and washed 'em all back. The funny thing was, that little one that got caught, she was a real fighter. She wouldn't give up. They put her in a dam so they could breed from her, but one day it rained so much the dam wall broke, she ended up back in the river. She was washed all the way downstream to the mouth of the river. Down to where the fish had come from. Back with her mob.

PEARL: Was that where the fresh water met the sea?

PAT: I knew you'd come back.

*They hug.*

PEARL: Can't swim into a strong current forever. It's very tiring!

PAT: Yeah.

PEARL: What are you doing here?

PAT: Keepin' an eye on things.

PEARL: Oh? You?

PAT: Turned over a new leaf. Didn't do such a good job last time, did I?

PEARL: How is she?

PAT: Surviving.

PEARL: I only found out… I thought…

PAT: She won't come down here.

PEARL: I'm not sure I'm ready…

PAT: I go up once a month. Keep an eye on her, grab some tucker…

PEARL: Does she ask after me?

PAT: She's never forgot you, bub.

PEARL: It's all really weird…

PAT: Yep.

PEARL: I'd kind of put all that behind me. I'd reconciled my past, but now…

PAT: All blackfellas got that problem.

PEARL: Will you tell her you've seen me?

PAT: She wanted me to leave you alone.

PEARL: But if—

PAT: She knew you were in a pretty good paddock.

PEARL: If I'd have known she was alive…

PAT: You would've bolted.

PEARL: Of course.

PAT: She thought you'd be better off where you were. That's why I waited for you to come.

PEARL: [*hugging him*] I've missed you, Uncle Pat…

PAT: Yeah. Look, I'm headin' up to see her in a few weeks. You could come with me.

PEARL: I… um… I'm not sure. Not yet. All this… phew!

PAT: When you're ready.

PEARL: It's really hard, Uncle Pat. You think your mother's dead, you adopt another family, you find out she's not dead… It's pretty wild.

PAT: So… what happened to the big office in the city?

PEARL: I couldn't handle the view.

PAT: She's a bit different down here.

PEARL: What am I going to do about Mrs Gorrie? They'll lock the boy up…

PAT: Why don't we go down and get him out?

PEARL: They'll want family…

PAT: Hey! We're family.

PEARL: Yes but—

PAT: One blackfella's the same as another to most whitefellas!

PEARL: It's a bit dodgy, Uncle Pat.

PAT: So? Won't do him no good, a night in the lock-up.

PEARL: No but…

PAT: You need a bit of 'educamating'.

PEARL: It's scary.

PAT: Yep.

PEARL: Will you help me?

PAT: 'Course.

PEARL: There's a bit of a hole…

PAT: I'll help you fill it, bub. [*He shadow boxes.*] Bouncin' back, duckin' and weavin', usin' the ropes. More than one way to skin a cat!

   *She laughs.*

PEARL: Come on, let's go and see what we can do for young Gorrie.

PAT: You driving?

PEARL: Here? You kidding? Didn't want my car knocked off, did I? You know what they say about you blackfellas.

PAT: Us.

PEARL: Us. [*She hails a cab.*] Taxi!

PAT: My shout.

PEARL: Toss you for it.

> PAT *takes out a coin.*

No way! [*She takes out a coin.*] My lucky shilling. Remember?

> *She tosses it.*

PAT: Heads!

PEARL: [*inspecting the coin*] Bad luck, Uncle Pat, it's a tail! Taxi!

◆ ◆ ◆ ◆ ◆

*SCENE TWELVE*

*1990. The bush. Evening.*

ANNIE *is chasing chooks away with her broom. Her baby doll is on the ground beside her.*

ANNIE: Bloody chooks! Get out of here. Go on. Get out of it. Get back to your yard. What do you think this is? Messin' up my yard. You don't belong out here. You know that! Go on. Get back where you belong. I'll sool them mangy dogs on to you. I will. Get back in there and lay a few decent eggs for a change.

> *She continues to sweep, then picks up the doll and sits it on a box.*

Can't be bothered. Can't be bothered anymore. [*She sits the doll down in front of her.*] I'm no bloody good to you anymore. No I'm not. Look at me. Look at me, girl.

> *She buries her head in her hands, ruffles her hair and then pats the doll gently. She tells a bedtime story.*

Funny, gettin' older. Your life starts flashing past you. It's like you're sittin' in the train and you look out the window at everything…

Voom! voom! voom! [*She snaps her head to indicate.*] Your mind goes back and forth, things jump out at you, suprise you. You don't know what's real and what isn't. It all ends up in a big melting pot. Some things get jumbled. Other things come back plain as day. I try to only remember the good things but… your mind… gets all muddied up.

Ahh, I'm too old to dwell on the pain. I've had the pain and I've had the good times, plenty of 'em too, don't you worry, missy! I try and think about them but… who am I kidding? You never forget. No matter how hard you try, you never forget. You live with the memories… you can't shake your past.

As for me, bubby, I've had enough. Time for me to move on, to let someone else have a turn. Time for me to call it a day. I've had enough of all this… this… [*She puts the doll under the box.*] Them chooks, they're lucky, they'll get eaten before they get too old. I'm gonna lie down and go to sleep and hope I never wake up, that's what I'm going to do. [*She lies down, pulling an old blanket over her head.*] No bloody noise, you lot. Leave me to me dreams.

*The light fades. The sounds of the bush at nightfall. Peace and quiet. A torch flashes across the stage.* PAT *enters. He approaches warily.*

PAT: [*whispering*] Sis?

*Silence.*

Sis!

*He freezes. He approaches her. There is no response.*

Hell no!

*He leans over, trying to stir the body.*

Oh God! Wake up please! [*He stares.*] Oh no… don't… don't tell me…

*Suddenly* ANNIE *throws the blanket off her.*

ANNIE: What's all the racket for? Can't a person die in peace around here?

PAT: Hooley dooley!

ANNIE: What are you staring at?

PAT: I thought… for a minute there…

ANNIE: Got ya, eh?

PAT: I knew you were havin' me on.

ANNIE: Bull, you thought I'd carked it, didn't you?

PAT: Listen, sis…

ANNIE: Leave me alone.

PAT: I've got some news for you.

ANNIE: Go away! I don't want no news…

> *She wraps the blanket around herself and turns away.* PAT *drags the blanket off her. They struggle.*

Get away from me!

PAT: It's all right.

ANNIE: What do you want?

PAT: Calm down.

ANNIE: Bugger off!

PAT: Stop it, sis.

ANNIE: I don't need you.

PAT: Don't keep saying that.

ANNIE: You're dead as far as I'm concerned.

PAT: Oh hell, sis! I seen Pearl.

ANNIE: You told me.

PAT: No. I seen her. I talked to her.

ANNIE: I told you to leave her alone.

PAT: Listen!

ANNIE: Don't you tell me—

PAT: She needs to see you.

ANNIE: No.

PAT: I want you to come with me.

ANNIE: No.

PAT: To town. She's in at the motel. She was gonna come but—

ANNIE: I'm not goin' nowhere. I know what you'll do. You'll put me away.

PAT: She—

> PEARL *enters.* PAT *sees her.*

PEARL: Mum?

ANNIE *turns and stares.*

Mum?

ANNIE: Mum?

PEARL: I couldn't wait any longer.

PAT: Good on ya, bub.

PEARL: Is this…?

PAT: Uh-huh.

ANNIE: She's not…

PAT: She is, sis…

ANNIE: You, girl?

PEARL: Yes.

ANNIE: You my girl?

PEARL: Yes. It's me. Pearl.

ANNIE: No…

PAT: True.

ANNIE: You?

PEARL: Yes.

ANNIE: Oh…

    *She stumbles.* PAT *supports her.*

It's Pearl?

PAT: Yes.

ANNIE: Here?

PEARL: Yes, Mum.

ANNIE: You come here?

PEARL: Yes.

ANNIE: To me?

PEARL: Mmm.

ANNIE: Ohhh…

PAT: You right, sis?

ANNIE: Come here, girl. Come here.

    PEARL *approaches.*

Come…

    *She beckons her with outstretched arms.* PAT *slips back into the shadows.*

PEARL: Mu—

ANNIE: Look.
PEARL: Yes?
ANNIE: Look at you.
PEARL: Oh, Mum…
ANNIE: Let me touch you. My Pearl.
PEARL: Oh, dear God…
ANNIE: My baby…
PEARL: Yes… your baby…
ANNIE: Ohh, look at you, you're so pretty. Are you really my baby girl?
   My little baby?
PEARL: I am.
ANNIE: My baby's come home to me.
PAT: She has, sis.
ANNIE: My Pearl. My beautiful little Pearl.

   ANNIE *and* PEARL *hug. Suddenly* ANNIE *pushes her away.*

What are you doin' dressed like that? You look terrible. Where's
your shame…?
PEARL: Thanks, Mum.
PAT: Told you she hasn't changed.
ANNIE: What are you grinning at, you bloody ratbag?!
PAT: You!
ANNIE: Get here…
PAT: Don't you hit me!
ANNIE: Hit you? Where's that bloody stick?

## THE END